MEDITERRANEAN

a taste of the sun in over 150 recipes

MEDITERRANEAN

a taste of the sun in over 150 recipes

JACQUELINE CLARK and JOANNA FARROW

HERMES HOUSE

This edition published by Hermes House in 2003

© Anness Publishing Limited 1996, 2003

Hermes House is an imprint of
Anness Publishing Limited
Hermes House
88–89 Blackfriars Road
London SE1 8HA

A CIP catalogue record for this book is available from the British Library.

Publisher: Joanna Lorenz
Senior Cookery Editor: Linda Fraser
Designer: Nigel Partridge
Photography and styling: Michelle Garrett, assisted by Dulce Riberio
Food for photography: Jacqueline Clark and Joanna Farrow
Illustrator: Anna Koska

Front cover shows Black Pasta with Squid Sauce. For recipe see page 114.
Previously published as *Taste of the Mediterranean*

3 5 7 9 10 8 6 4 2

NOTES
For all recipes, quantities are given in both metric and imperial measures and, where
appropriate, measures are also given in standard cups and spoons.
Follow one set, but not a mixture, because they are not interchangeable.
Standard spoon and cup measures are level.
1 tsp = 5ml, 1 tbsp = 15ml, 1 cup = 250ml/8fl oz
Australian standard tablespoons are 20ml. Australian readers should use 3 tsp in place of 1 tbsp for
measuring small quantities of gelatine, cornflour, salt, etc.
Medium eggs are used unless otherwise stated.

CONTENTS

INTRODUCTION

*The countries bounded by the Mediterranean sea
produce some of the finest food the world has to
offer — set sail with us on a culinary tour.*

ABOVE: A grove of old olive trees lit by the afternoon sun in Provence.

Azure skies, even bluer seas, white-gold sands, bright, whitewashed walls, the vibrant reds, greens, yellows, purples and oranges of the flowers, fruit and vegetables on display in the market – these are the paint palette colours of the Mediterranean. These evocative images are familiar to many of us, although, of course, we will not all be thinking of the same country – after all, there are fifteen to consider, surrounding the sea itself. A quick tour will take us from the shores of Spain, to France, Italy, Greece, Turkey, Syria, Lebanon, Israel, and into Africa to Egypt, Libya, Tunisia, Algeria and Morocco. The islands of Malta and Cyprus are truly Mediterranean, encircled by the sea. In many ways these fifteen countries are completely different from each other, but one thread links them all – the love of good food.

Centuries before Christ, the area surrounding the Mediterranean sea was colonized by the Phoenicians, Greeks and Romans, who shared a basic cultivation of wheat, olives and grapes. These, in turn, became bread, oil and wine, three components which are still very important in today's Mediterranean diet. With the building of ships came import and export, and the various countries began a cross-pollination of crops, ingredients and recipes. Spices and flavourings were introduced through North Africa and Arabia, and saffron, cloves, chillies, ginger and allspice continue to be popular all over the Mediterranean, appearing in sweet and savoury dishes. Nuts, too, are an ingredient common to many of the countries. Almonds, pistachio and pine nuts are perhaps the most popular as they are native to the region.

When thinking of Mediterranean food, however, it is the fresh fruit, vegetables and herbs which immediately spring to mind. Open-air markets from Marseilles to Morocco are a feast for the senses. Fabulous arrays of

tomatoes, aubergines, courgettes, peaches, figs, garlic and pungent herbs such as basil and thyme are tantalizingly displayed; the experience being made complete by the hot sun, drawing out the flavours and smells. Mediterranean cooking depends on the freshest of ingredients; it is honest, simple and prepared with respect.

Recent research has proved the Mediterranean diet to be a very healthy one thus increasing its popularity. Olive oil is at the heart of this theory; used in cooking, it contains a high proportion of mono-unsaturated fats. Olive oils vary in colour, from the golden Spanish varieties to the deep greens of some Greek, Provençal and Italian oils. Colour is not really an indication of quality; the oils have to be tasted, and flavour, like colour, varies immensely.

BELOW: Glossy green leaves shade juicy oranges in a grove near Seville.

ABOVE: Watermelons and other gourds lie piled in the sun in a Greek market.

The people of the Mediterranean have known great hardship. Although we have holiday images of sunny days, the weather can be wild and unjust. Lack of rain, terrible winds and a capricious sea ruin crops and the fishermen's haul; in the past, foreign domination and disease caused poverty and death. Because of this, the most basic foods are, even today, a celebration of life to the Mediterranean people. Bread is an important staple and always accompanies a meal, be it a bowl of soup or a platter of grilled fish.

Perhaps Mediterranean food could be described as "peasant food", not in a derogatory sense, but as a homage to the people who have provided and inspired us with such a vast and wonderful repertoire of recipes, ancient and new. In this book, we give you just a few of the countless dishes from around the Mediterranean shores. Some are traditional, for example, Gazpacho soup, Ratatouille, Greek Salad and Provençal Beef Daube, while others are more contemporary, using Mediterranean ingredients but creating something new. Amongst these recipes are Grilled Vegetable Terrine, Pan-fried Red Mullet with Basil and Citrus, Mushroom and Pesto Pizza, and Turkish Delight Ice Cream.

As in the Mediterranean, ingredients should be fresh and of the highest quality, even if this means waiting for some of them, such as clams or figs, to be in season. We hope to bring you a true taste of the Mediterranean.

INGREDÍENTS

VEGETABLES

ARTICHOKES There are two types of artichoke, in no way related: the globe, which belongs to the thistle family, and the Jerusalem, which is a tuber, belonging to the sunflower family. The globe artichoke is common throughout the Mediterranean, appearing as different varieties, depending on the country. When buying, choose firm, taut specimens. After boiling, the leaves and base are edible. Baby varieties are completely edible and are sometimes eaten raw. Jerusalem artichokes look like knobbly potatoes, and can be treated as such.

AUBERGINES Although aubergines originated from Asia they feature in dishes from every Mediterranean country. There are many different varieties, including green, white and yellow, but the plump purple variety is the most common. Look for firm, taut, shiny-skinned specimens with green stalks. Aubergines are sometimes salted and drained before cooking, which helps to extract bitter juices and makes them absorb less oil during cooking.

BROAD OR FAVA BEANS These beans are often imported from various Mediterranean countries in the Spring before we enjoy our own. When young, they can be cooked and eaten, pods and all, or shelled and eaten raw with

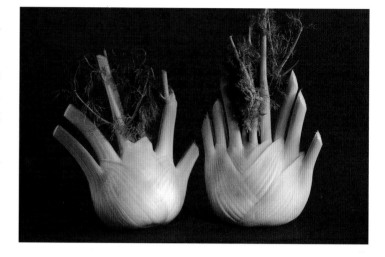

Fennel

Artichokes

cheese, as in Italy. When the beans are older, they are shelled, cooked, and sometimes peeled. Dried broad beans are popular in the Middle East where they are cooked with spices or added to stews.

COURGETTES These baby marrows are at their best when they are small. They can be eaten raw, and have a good flavour and crisp texture. The larger they become, the less flavour they have. When buying, choose firm, shiny specimens. Yellow varieties are sometimes available and, although there is no difference in flavour, they make a pretty alternative to the usual green variety. In Italy and France, the golden courgette flowers are stuffed and cooked, or deep-fried in batter.

FENNEL This white bulb of overlapping leaves and green, feathery fronds has a fresh aniseed flavour and can be eaten cooked or raw. Its flavour complements fish and chicken, but it is also delicious served as a separate vegetable course either roasted, or baked with a cheese sauce. Choose firm, rounded bulbs, and use the fronds for garnishing. If using raw, toss the slices in lemon juice to prevent them from discoloring.

MUSHROOMS The varieties used in Mediterranean cooking are button, open cup and flat, but regional wild species,

Okra

such as ceps, chanterelles and oyster mushrooms are to be found in the markets during autumn.

OKRA This unusual vegetable, sometimes called lady's fingers, is a long five-sided green pod, with a tapering end. It has a subtle flavour and a gelatinous texture which helps to thicken and enrich certain dishes. Used in Middle Eastern and Greek cookery, its most successful partners are garlic, onion and tomatoes. Choose small, firm specimens and use sliced or whole in cooking.

ONIONS The starting point of so many dishes, the onion is invaluable to Mediterranean cooking. There are many varieties, differing in colour, size and strength of flavour. For salads, or when onion is to be used raw, choose red or white-skinned varieties which have a sweet, mild flavour. The large, Spanish onions have a mild flavour too, and are a good choice when a large quantity of onion is called for in a recipe. Baby onions are perfect for adding whole to stews, or serving as a vegetable dish on their own.

PEPPERS Sweet peppers add colour to markets across the Mediterranean region. To make the most of their flavour, grill peppers until the skins are charred, then rub off and discard the skins. Marinate the peppers in olive oil.

RADICCHIO This red chicory is very popular in Italy. There are several varieties, but the most common is the round variety which looks like a little lettuce. The leaves are crisp and pleasantly bitter and can be eaten raw or cooked. Radicchio is delicious grilled and drizzled with olive oil and sprinkled with black pepper, or shredded and stirred into risotto or spaghetti. The raw leaves make a colourful addition to salads.

RADISHES These are best eaten raw to appreciate their peppery flavour – serve them as the French do, with salt and butter or use them as a colourful addition to a platter of *crudités*.

SPINACH This leaf vegetable is very popular in the Mediterranean countries. Cooked or raw, it is a good source of vitamins A and C. Young spinach leaves can be eaten raw and need little preparation, but older leaves should be washed in several changes of water and then picked over and the tough stalks removed. Spinach is used in Middle Eastern pastries, Spanish tapas, French tarts and many more dishes – eggs and fish, for instance, make good partners. A little doesn't go a long way – if the spinach is to be cooked, allow 250g/9oz raw weight per person.

Radishes

Vine tomatoes

TOMATOES Some of the best tomatoes are to be found in Mediterranean markets. Sun-ripened and full of flavour, they come in many varieties – beef-steak tomatoes for stuffing, plum tomatoes, vine tomatoes, cherry tomatoes and baby pear-shaped ones. Cooked with onion and garlic, tomatoes make the universal sauce that so many Mediterranean dishes rely on. Canned and sun-dried tomatoes are invaluable items to keep in the store cupboard.

VINE LEAVES These pretty leaves have been used in cooking for hundreds of years. They can be stuffed with a variety of fillings and also make perfect wrappers for meat, fish and poultry. Fresh leaves must be young and soft. If using brined vine leaves, soak them in hot water for 20–30 minutes before stuffing or wrapping.

OLIVES

The fruit of one of the earliest known trees native to the Mediterranean. There are hundreds of varieties, differing widely in size, quality and taste. Colour depends purely on ripeness – the fruit changes from yellow to green, violet, purple, brown and finally black when fully ripened. Fresh olives are picked at the desired stage of ripeness, then soaked in water, bruised and immersed in brine to produce the familiar-tasting result. They can be bought whole or pitted, sometimes stuffed with peppers, anchovies or nuts, or bottled with flavourings such as garlic, coriander, chilli and herbs.

DAIRY PRODUCE

CHEESE The range of cheeses from Mediterranean countries is diverse – varieties are made from cow's, goat's, ewe's and, in the case of Italian mozzarella, buffalo's milk. Cream cheese is also common to many countries, varying a little according to the milk and the method used for preparing it.

YOGURT This live product (pasteurized milk combined with two beneficial bacteria) is perhaps most associated with the Middle Eastern countries, where it is used extensively in cooking. Greek yogurt is thick and creamy, and French yogurt is traditionally of the set variety. It is used as a marinade, a dip and to enrich soups and stews, and can be made from goat's, ewe's or cow's milk.

GRAINS

COUSCOUS This is a product made from semolina. The grains have been rolled, dampened and coated with the fine wheat flour. The commercial variety simply needs moistening, then steaming to swell the grains and produce a soft texture. It is the staple of the North African diet and is usually served with a spicy meat or vegetable stew, but it can also be used as a stuffing or in salads.

CRACKED WHEAT Also known as bulgur wheat, this cereal has been partially processed, and so cooks quickly. It can be used in place of rice as an accompaniment to grilled meats, as a stuffing, mixed with minced meat to make patties, or in salads, such as *tabbouleh*.

RICE There are many varieties of this world-wide staple food. In Italy there are at least four short-grained types used for risotto, and in Spain, Valencia rice is the preferred variety for *paella*. In the Middle East it is served with every meal, either plainly boiled or cooked with saffron and spices to create fragrant *pilaus*.

FRUIT

DATES Although fresh dates are quite widely available, imported from Israel and California, the dried variety remains an invaluable addition to cakes and tea-breads. Fresh dates should be plump and slightly wrinkled and

Sea bass

have a rich honey-like flavour and dense texture. They are best treated simply, or stoned and served with thick Greek yogurt.

FIGS This fruit is associated with all the Mediterranean countries. Different varieties vary in colour, from dark purple to green to a golden yellow, but all are made up of hundreds of tiny seeds, surrounded by soft pink flesh which is perfectly edible. Choose firm unblemished fruit, which just yield to the touch. Treat them simply, or serve with Parma ham or Greek yogurt and honey.

MELONS This fruit comes in many different sizes, shapes and colours – cantaloupe, charentais, galia, honeydew, ogen, orange- and green-fleshed varieties, and the wonderful pink watermelon. Ripe melons should yield to gentle pressure at the stalk end and have a fragrant scent. Rarely used in cooked dishes, they are best eaten chilled, by the slice, or as part of a fruit salad.

PEACHES AND NECTARINES Peaches need plenty of sun to ripen them and grow in France, Spain and Italy. There are yellow-, pink- and white-fleshed varieties. Some are cling, where the flesh clings to the stone, others are of the freestone variety. Look for bruise-free specimens that just give when squeezed gently. Nectarines are smooth-

Figs

skinned, with all the luscious flavour of the peach.

ORANGES This fruit is grown all over the Mediterranean, particularly in Spain. Seville oranges, the bitter marmalade variety, have a short season in January. The best of the flavour comes from the zest – the outer layer of the skin and this is often included in recipes using oranges.

FISH AND SHELLFISH

RED MULLET Very popular along the coasts of the Mediterranean, the red mullet is a pretty fish. It is usually treated simply by grilling over a wood fire, often with the liver still inside to add flavour. It can also be filleted and pan-fried, or included in delicious fish soups.

SEA BASS This is quite an expensive fish and is usually sold and cooked whole. The flesh is soft and delicate and needs careful attention when cooking. Methods include poaching, steaming, grilling and baking.

SQUID Very popular in the Mediterranean, particularly in Spain, Italy and Portugal. Squid vary in size from the tiny specimens that can be eaten whole, to the larger varieties, which are good for stuffing, grilling or stewing. The flesh is sweet and, when cooked for a short time, tender. Long cooking will also produce succulent results. Sometimes the ink is used to make a sauce for the squid.

SALT COD Most salt cod is prepared in Norway, Iceland and Newfoundland and then exported to Mediterranean countries. It is gutted, cleaned and soaked in brine, then dried. The end result looks very unappetizing, with a pungent smell, but after soaking for 48 hours and

cooking in the Mediterranean style, it is delicious.

TUNA An oily fish belonging to the same family as the mackerel. The flesh, which is sold in steaks or large pieces, is dark red and very dense, and has a tendency to dry out when cooked. Marinating before cooking helps to keep the flesh moist as does basting while cooking. Tuna can be baked, fried, grilled or stewed.

CRAB There are thousands of species of crab around the world. In the Mediterranean countries, brown and spider crabs are the most common. The meat of the crab is divided into two sorts – brown and white. Crabs are often sold cooked and dressed, which means that the crab has been prepared and is ready to eat. Choose heavy cooked crabs which should have a lot of meat.

MUSSELS Available in the Mediterranean from September to April, mussels usually need to be scrubbed and have the beard – the hairy tuft attached to the shell – removed. Any open mussels should be discarded if they do not close after a sharp tap. Mussels vary in size and the shell can be blue-black to dappled brown. They are easy to cook – just steam for a few minutes in a covered pan.

PRAWNS These vary enormously in size. The classic Mediterranean prawn is large, about 20cm/8in, reddish brown in colour when raw, and pink when cooked. When prawns are cooked over a fierce heat, such as a barbecue, the shell is often left on to protect the flesh from charring.

PULSES

CHICK-PEAS This pulse looks like a pale golden hazelnut and is sold either dried or ready cooked. Chick-peas have a nutty flavour and are used in stews from North Africa to Spain. In the Middle East they are

Prawns

made into flour, and in Greece they are puréed to produce a delicious dip. Soak them for at least 5 hours before cooking. They may have to be cooked for up to 4 hours, before they become tender. This varies according to the age of the chick-peas.

HARICOT BEANS These small plump white beans, which are quite soft when cooked, are used in casseroles in Spain and Portugal, as well as the famous *cassoulet* from France. They need to be soaked for 3–4 hours before cooking, and are also good in soups and salads.

LENTILS These come in different sizes and can be yellow, red, brown or green. The tiny green Puy lentils are favoured in France and the brown and red ones in the Middle East where they are cooked with spices to make dhals. They are also used in soups and need no soaking time, cooking in under an hour.

PASTA

Pasta is simply the Latin word for "paste", the flour-and-egg-based dough from which it is made. Although a staple of Italian cooking, pasta is widely used throughout the Mediterranean and has much in common with Chinese noodles which filtered from China via the Middle-Eastern trade routes. In Italy today there are countless varieties, from flat sheets of lasagne and ribbon noodles to pressed and moulded shapes, specifically designed to pocket substantial amounts of the sauce they are served with. Dried pasta shapes make a good standby, but fresh has a better flavour and texture and freezes well. Both can be bought flavoured with tomato, olive, spinach or mushroom paste. Black pasta, made with the addition of

Toasted pine nuts

squid ink, is increasingly popular. Home-made pasta is easy to make if time is allowed for chilling the fresh dough. Rolling it can be done effortlessly using a pasta machine.

NUTS

ALMONDS Cultivated commercially in Spain, Italy and Portugal, the almond is widely used in the Arab-influenced countries. It is an important ingredient in sweet pastries and is often added to savoury dishes, too. Almonds are sold fresh in their green velvety shells in the Mediterranean markets.

PINE NUTS These little nuts are used in both sweet and savoury dishes, and are one of the principal ingredients in pesto, the basil sauce from Italy.

PISTACHIO NUTS This colourful nut originated in the Middle East. It has flesh which ranges from pale to dark green, and a papery, purple-tinged skin. Pistachio nuts have a subtle flavour and are used in a wide range of dishes, from pastries (both sweet and savoury) to ice creams and nougat.

WALNUTS This very versatile nut is used in both sweet and savoury dishes. Walnut oil is a popular addition to salad dressings in France. Elsewhere, walnuts are chopped and added to pastries, ground to make sauces, or eaten fresh as "wet" walnuts.

HERBS

BASIL One of the herbs most crucial to Mediterranean cooking, particularly in Italian dishes. The sweet tender leaves, sometimes each as large as a cabbage leaf, have a great affinity with tomatoes, aubergines, peppers, courgettes and cheese. A handful of torn leaves enlivens a green salad, and can be packed into a bottle of olive oil to produce an aromatic flavour.

BAY These hardy leaves are taken from the bay shrub or tree and are widely used to flavour slow-cooked recipes like stocks, soups and stews. They are also added to marinades, threaded on to kebab skewers, thrown on the barbecue to invigorate the smoky flavour, or used for decorative purposes. One or two young bay leaves, infused with milk or cream in puddings, add a warm, pungent flavour.

BOUQUET GARNI A collection of herbs that classically includes parsley, thyme and bay, although other herbs like rosemary and marjoram can be added. Available dried, tied in muslin bundles or in "teabag-like" sachets. Fresh bouquet garni can be tied together with string for easy removal from the dish before serving.

CHERVIL This delicate, pretty-leafed, gentle herb is rather like a mild parsley and needs to be used generously to impart sufficient flavour. Widely used in French cooking, it works well in herb butters and with eggs and cheese.

CHIVES A grass-like herb which produces a beautiful purplish flower. Its flavour resembles mild onions.

CORIANDER Huge bundles of fresh coriander are a familiar sight in Eastern Mediterranean markets, their warm, pungent aroma rising at the merest touch. The leaves impart a distinctive flavour to soups, stews, sauces and spicy dishes when added towards the end of cooking. They are also used sparingly in salads and yogurt dishes.

DILL Feathery dill leaves have a mild aniseed taste, popular in the Eastern Mediterranean, particularly Greece and Turkey. It is chopped into fish and chicken dishes, as well as stuffings and rice. Pickled gherkins and cucumbers are often flavoured with dill.

MARJORAM A versatile herb of which there are several varieties. It grows both wild and cultivated and goes very well with red meats, game and tomato dishes. Oregano is a wild form of marjoram.

Basket of herbs

MINT One of the oldest and most widely used herbs. In Greece, chopped mint accompanies other herbs to enhance stuffed vegetables and fish dishes, and in Turkey and the Middle East finely chopped mint adds a cooling tang to yogurt dishes as well as teas and iced drinks.

PARSLEY Flat leaf parsley is far more widely used in Mediterranean cookery than the tightly curled variety. Mixed with garlic and lemon zest, it makes a wonderfully aromatic *gremolata*, a colourful, refreshing garnish for scattering over tomato and rice dishes.

ROSEMARY Cut from the pretty flowering shrub, rosemary grows well throughout the Mediterranean and is most widely used in meat cookery. Several sprigs, tucked under a roast chicken or lamb with plenty of garlic, impart an inviting warm, sweet flavour.

SAGE Native to the Northern Mediterranean, soft, velvety sage leaves have a strong, distinctive flavour and should be used sparingly in meat and game dishes. Sage can be added to stuffings or pan-fried with pigeon and liver to give an interesting flavour.

TARRAGON Long, lank tarragon leaves have a very individual aroma and flavour, most widely appreciated in French cookery. It is used generously in egg and chicken dishes, and with salmon and trout. Tarragon-flavoured vinegar makes a delicious ingredient of a good mayonnaise or Hollandaise sauce.

THYME A few sprigs of hardy thyme add a warm, earthy flavour to slow-cooked meat and poultry dishes as well as to pâtés, marinades and vegetable dishes.

SPICES

CARDAMOM Usually associated with Indian cookery, the use of cardamom extends to the Eastern Mediterranean. The black, green or white pods should be pounded to release the small black seeds which can be bruised to accentuate the flavour. The pods are usually discarded.

CHILLIES These are the small fiery relatives of the sweet pepper family. Mediterranean chillies are generally milder in flavour than the unbearably fiery South American ones but should still be used with caution as their heat is difficult to gauge. It is the oil in chillies that accounts for the heat and the irritation they can cause to sensitive skin.

CINNAMON Cinnamon sticks, the thin curled bark of the cinnamon tree, have an aromatic, sweet flavour that is used extensively in the Eastern Mediterranean to flavour meat and *pilau* dishes, and to infuse milk and syrups for puddings. Ground cinnamon is more convenient but lacks the fresh, sweet flavour.

CORIANDER SEEDS The seeds of the coriander herb have a warm, slightly orange flavour that is essential to many dishes of the Eastern Mediterranean. Their flavour can be accentuated by crushing and gently heating them in a frying pan before using.

CUMIN SEEDS These dark, spindly shaped seeds are often married with coriander when making spicy dishes that are typical of North Africa and the Eastern Mediterranean.

MACE This is the thin, lacy covering of nutmeg, available ground to a powder or as thin "blades". It has a gentler flavour than nutmeg.

NUTMEG Nutmeg's beautiful, sweet warm aroma makes a good addition to sweet and savoury dishes, particularly with spinach, cheese, eggs, terrines and pâtés.

PEPPER There are several different types of peppercorns, all of which are picked from the pepper vine, a plant unrelated to the capsicum family. Black peppercorns have the strongest flavour. Green peppercorns are the fresh unripe berries which are bottled while soft.

Preserved lemons

SAFFRON This is by far the most highly prized spice, since it takes the hand-picked stamens of about 70,000 saffron crocuses to make up 450g/1lb of the spice. Its exotic, rich colour and flavour is indispensable in many Mediterranean dishes, particularly French fish stews, Spanish rice and chicken dishes and Italian risottos. To accentuate the flavour the strands are best lightly crushed and soaked in a little boiling water before use.

FLAVOURINGS

CAPERS Capers are the pickled buds of a shrub native to the Mediterranean region. The best are those preserved in salt rather than brine or vinegar. When capers are roughly chopped, their sharp piquant tang is used to cut the richness of lamb, enliven fish sauces and flavour salads and pastes such as *tapenade.*

GARLIC Sold in "strings" or as separate bulbs, the main consideration when buying garlic is that the cloves are plump and firm. Garlic is one of the most vital ingredients in Mediterranean cookery and there are few recipes in which its addition would be out of place. Used crushed, sliced or even whole, garlic develops a smooth, gentle flavour with long slow cooking. Used raw in salads, mayonnaise and sauce, garlic has a hot, fierce impact.

HARISSA A fiery hot paste used mostly in North African cookery. It is made from a blend of chillies, garlic, cumin, coriander and cayenne and can be bought in small jars.

HONEY An ancient sweetener that depends on the flowers on which the bees have fed for its individual fragrance and flavour. The Turks and Greeks use it in their syrupy pastries and puddings and small quantities are added to some savoury dishes.

LEMONS AND LIMES The grated rind or squeezed juice of lemons and limes are widely added to fish, meat and poultry for a typically fresh flavour.

ORANGE RIND Thinly pared strips of orange rind give a fresh fragrance, particularly in the fish stews and soups of southern France.

PRESERVED LEMONS AND LIMES Lemons or limes preserved in salt develop a mellow flavour, much used in Mediterranean dishes. To make them, scrub and quarter almost through to the base and rub cut sides with salt. Pack tightly into a large sterilized jar. Half fill the jar with more salt, adding some bay leaves, peppercorns and cinnamon if liked. Cover completely with lemon juice. Cover with a lid and store for two weeks, shaking the jar daily. Add a little olive oil to seal and use within one to six months, washing off the salt before use.

ROSE WATER This distilled essence of rose petals is used mainly in Eastern Mediterranean desserts, giving a mild rose fragrance and flavour. The strength varies greatly so add carefully at first.

TAHINI A smooth oily paste ground from sesame seeds and used to give a nutty flavour to Middle Eastern dishes.

TOMATO PURÉE A concentrated paste made from fresh tomatoes, perfect for boosting the flavour of bland tomatoes in soups, stews and sauces. Use sun-dried tomato paste for a richer, riper flavour.

OLIVE OIL

Besides its healthy qualities, olive oil is indispensable to mediterranean cooking for its fine, nutty flavour. Italy, France and Spain produce some of the best. The richest oil comes from the first cold pressing of the olives, producing a rich green "virgin" oil.

APPETIZERS

There is a splendid array of appetizers to be enjoyed throughout the Mediterranean. The variety of flavours makes them irresistible.

LEFT: *On the mountainous Greek island of Naxos, arable land is precious, and hillsides are extensively terraced.*

"Tapas", "Apéritifs", "Mezze", "Mezedes" – all these terms describe the inexhaustible and highly flavoured range of appetizers or nibbles that are served with drinks before a meal or as a light snack at almost any time of day. This is one of the most enticing aspects of Mediterranean cookery; the irresistible "tasters" enjoyed in a casual, unhurried atmosphere, offering a culinary glimpse of the good things to follow. For the cook, the preparation of these savouries can be as simple or as demanding as time and circumstances allow. Whether it is a selection of marinated olives, regional cheeses or fresh seafood or, on a more elaborate scale, delicious baked vegetables, pickles and spicy pastries, this informal style of enjoying food is quintessentially Mediterranean.

In Spanish, "tapa" means a lid and it was the custom

RIGHT: Bent double, Moroccan farm workers bring in the olive harvest.

of bartenders serving glasses of sherry covered with a slice of sausage or ham which evolved into the most fascinating and imaginative selection of "little dishes" served today. Tapas bars, particularly abundant in southern Spain, serve a variety of such dishes. In these bars you can enjoy pre-dinner tasters or thoroughly indulge yourself with a selection of dishes as a main meal. Fried new potatoes, chorizo sausage in olive oil, garlic prawns and empanadillas are tapas classics. Tortilla, an omelette in which fried potatoes are layered in a pan, covered with beaten eggs and baked to a set "cake" is another well-established dish. It is served warm or cold, cut into wedges, washed down with local chilled wines or, like other tapas, with sherry, port or beer.

In the Eastern Mediterranean, in places like Turkey, Greece, Lebanon and North Africa, local and specialized variations of a mezze are popular with both locals and visitors. Arak, raki and ouzo, as well as wine, are drunk with a wonderful selection of appetizers to whet the appetite. These are usually highly spiced and aromatic. In Greece, sheep's and goat's yogurt are hung to produce thickened cheeses that are bottled in spiced olive oil. Spread on to warmed toast, this delicious snack is good

ABOVE: Scales at the ready, a Turkish fisherman sets out his catch on his stall.

enough to enjoy as a complete meal. Dressed tomatoes, fried Halloumi or Keflotyri cheese drizzled with lemon juice and pepper and a bowl of garlic-flavoured Greek yogurt complete a mouthwatering spread.

Vegetables, salads and pulses feature highly on a North African or Lebanese mezze. Simple vegetable *crudités* such as carrots, turnips and cucumber are scattered with coarse salt and left to marinate lightly before being moistened with lemon juice or wine vinegar. Miniature versions of national dishes such as *kibbeh* and little filo pastries are also ideal for whetting the appetite.

Sampling a selection of nibbles before a Turkish meal is almost compulsory and the range of dishes is very extensive. A rich, thick sauce of chilli tomatoes and a refreshing Cacik provide a stimulating contrast alongside specialities such as garlic mussels, grilled vegetables and stuffed peppers.

The classic Italian appetizer is the "antipasto", usually an assortment of cured meats such as salami, prosciutto and other cured meats, served alongside roasted pepper salads, artichokes in olive oil, dressed green beans, anchovy fillets and breads such as crostini and focaccia.

Tasty dips like Tapenade, Herb Aïoli or a very garlicky French dressing are essential appetizers in France, often accompanied by a selection of raw or roasted *crudités*, herb salads and radishes with salt and butter.

Part of the pleasure of serving appetizers is that they can be as simple or as complicated as you like. Serve several as a light summer's meal, two or three as a simple starter or a varied selection for a larger party. Added interest can be provided, at little extra effort, with a variety of olives, interesting Mediterranean breads and salted or spiced nuts.

Essentially, plenty of time must be allowed so that the nibbles can be enjoyed in the unhurried and relaxed atmosphere that is an integral part of the Mediterranean way of life.

DEEP FRIED NEW POTATOES WITH SAFFRON AIOLI

Aïoli is a Spanish garlic mayonnaise, similar to the French mayonnaise of the same name. In this recipe saffron adds colour and flavour.

1 size 2 egg yolk
2.5ml/½ tsp Dijon mustard
300ml/½ pint/1¼ cups extra virgin
olive oil
15–30ml/1–2 tbsp lemon juice
1 garlic clove, crushed
2.5ml/½ tsp saffron strands
20 baby new potatoes
vegetable oil for frying
salt and ground black pepper

SERVES 4

1 To make the aïoli, put the egg yolk in a bowl with the mustard and a pinch of salt. Beat together with a wooden spoon. Still beating, add the olive oil very slowly, drop by drop to begin with, then, as the aïoli gradually thickens, in a thin stream. Add the lemon juice and salt and pepper to taste, then beat in the crushed garlic.

2 Place the saffron in a small bowl, and add 10ml/2 tsp hot water. Press the saffron with the back of a teaspoon, to extract the colour and flavour, and leave to infuse for 5 minutes. Beat the saffron and the liquid into the mayonnaise.

3 Cook the potatoes in boiling salted water for 5 minutes, then turn off the heat. Cover the pan and leave for 15 minutes. Drain the potatoes, then dry them thoroughly.

4 Heat 1cm/½in oil in a deep pan. When the oil is very hot, add the potatoes, and fry quickly, turning, until crisp and golden. Drain on kitchen paper, and serve with the saffron aïoli.

DATES STUFFED WITH CHORIZO

A delicious combination from Spain, using fresh dates and spicy chorizo sausage.

50g/2oz chorizo sausage
12 fresh dates, stoned
6 streaky bacon rashers
oil for frying
plain flour for dusting
1 egg, beaten
50g/2oz/1 cup fresh breadcrumbs
cocktail sticks for serving

SERVES 4–6

1 Trim the ends of the chorizo sausage and peel away the skin. Cut into three 2cm/¾in slices. Cut these in half lengthways, then into quarters, giving 12 pieces.

2 Stuff each date with a piece of chorizo, closing the date around it. Stretch the bacon, by running the back of a knife along the rasher. Cut each rasher in half, widthways. Wrap a piece of bacon around each date and secure with a cocktail stick.

3 In a deep pan, heat 1cm/½in of oil. Dust the dates with flour, dip them in the beaten egg, then coat in breadcrumbs. Fry the dates in the hot oil, turning them, until golden. Remove the dates with a slotted spoon, and drain on kitchen paper. Serve immediately.

SPINACH EMPANADILLAS

These are little pastry turnovers, filled with ingredients that have a strong Moorish influence — pine nuts and raisins.

25g/1oz/2 tbsp raisins
25ml/1½ tbsp olive oil
450g/1lb fresh spinach, washed
and chopped
6 drained canned anchovies, chopped
2 garlic cloves, finely chopped
25g/1oz/⅓ cup pine nuts, chopped
1 egg, beaten
350g/12oz puff pastry
salt and ground black pepper

MAKES 20

 1 To make the filling, soak the raisins in a little warm water for 10 minutes. Drain, then chop roughly. Heat the oil in a large sauté pan or wok, add the spinach, stir, then cover and cook over a low heat for about 2 minutes. Uncover, turn up the heat and let any liquid evaporate. Add the anchovies, garlic and seasoning. Cook, stirring, for a further minute. Remove from the heat, add the raisins and pine nuts, and cool.

2 Preheat the oven to 180°C/ 350°F/Gas 4. Roll out the pastry to a 3mm/⅛in thickness.

3 Using a 7.5cm/3in pastry cutter, cut out 20 rounds, re-rolling the dough if necessary. Place about two teaspoons of the filling in the middle of each round, then brush the edges with a little water. Bring up the sides of the pastry and seal well (*left*). Press the edges together with the back of a fork. Brush with egg. Place the turnovers on a lightly greased baking sheet and bake for about 15 minutes, until golden. Serve warm.

SAUTÉED MUSSELS WITH GARLIC AND HERBS

These mussels are served without their shells, in a delicious paprika flavoured sauce.
Eat them with cocktail sticks.

900g/2lb fresh mussels
1 lemon slice
90ml/6 tbsp olive oil
2 shallots, finely chopped
1 garlic clove, finely chopped
15ml/1 tbsp chopped fresh parsley
2.5ml/½ tsp sweet paprika
1.5ml/¼ tsp dried chilli flakes

SERVES 4

1 | Scrub the mussels, discarding any damaged ones that do not close when tapped with a knife. Put the mussels in a large pan, with 250ml/8fl oz/1 cup water, and the slice of lemon. Bring to the boil for 3–4 minutes and remove the mussels as they open. Discard any that remain closed. Take the mussels out of the shells and drain on kitchen paper.

2 | Heat the oil in a sauté pan, add the mussels, and cook, stirring, for a minute. Remove from the pan. Add the shallots and garlic and cook, covered, over a low heat, for about 5 minutes, until soft. Remove from the heat and stir in the parsley, paprika and chilli. Return to the heat and stir in the mussels with any juices. Cook briefly. Remove from the heat and cover for a minute or two, to let the flavours mingle, before serving.

TAPAS OF ALMONDS, OLIVES AND CHEESE

These three simple ingredients are lightly flavoured to create a delicious Spanish tapas medley that's perfect for a casual starter or nibbles to serve with pre-dinner drinks.

FOR THE MARINATED OLIVES
2.5ml/½ tsp coriander seeds
2.5ml/½ tsp fennel seeds
5ml/1 tsp chopped fresh rosemary
10ml/2 tsp chopped fresh parsley
2 garlic cloves, crushed
15ml/1 tbsp sherry vinegar
30ml/2 tbsp olive oil
115g/4oz/⅔ cup black olives
115g/4oz/⅔ cup green olives

FOR THE MARINATED CHEESE
150g/5oz goat's cheese, preferably
manchego
90ml/6 tbsp olive oil
15ml/1 tbsp white wine vinegar
5ml/1 tsp black peppercorns
1 garlic clove, sliced
3 fresh tarragon or thyme sprigs
tarragon sprigs, to garnish

FOR THE SALTED ALMONDS
1.5ml/¼ tsp cayenne pepper
30ml/2 tbsp sea salt
25g/1oz/2 tbsp butter
60ml/4 tbsp olive oil
200g/7oz/1¾ cups blanched almonds
extra salt for sprinkling (optional)

SERVES 6–8

1 To make the marinated olives, crush the coriander and fennel seeds with a pestle and mortar. Mix together with the rosemary, parsley, garlic, vinegar and oil and pour over the olives in a small bowl. Cover and chill for up to 1 week.

2 To make the marinated cheese, cut the cheese into bite-size pieces, leaving the rind on. Mix together the oil, vinegar, peppercorns, garlic and herb sprigs and pour over the cheese in a small bowl. Cover and chill for up to 3 days.

COOK'S TIP
If serving with pre-dinner drinks, provide cocktail sticks for spearing the olives and cheese.

3 To make the salted almonds, mix together the cayenne pepper and salt in a bowl. Melt the butter with the olive oil in a frying pan. Add the almonds to the pan and fry, stirring for about 5 minutes, until the almonds are golden.

4 Tip the almonds out of the frying pan, into the salt mixture and toss together until the almonds are coated. Leave to cool, then store them in a jar or airtight container for up to 1 week.

5 To serve the tapas, arrange in small, shallow serving dishes. Use fresh sprigs of tarragon to garnish the cheese and scatter the almonds with a little more salt, if liked.

ROASTED PEPPER ANTIPASTO

Jars of Italian mixed peppers in olive oil are now a common sight in many supermarkets. None, however, can compete with this colourful, freshly made version, perfect as a starter on its own, or with some Italian salamis and cold meats.

3 red peppers
2 yellow or orange peppers
2 green peppers
50g/2oz/½ cup sun-dried tomatoes in oil, drained
1 garlic clove
30ml/2 tbsp balsamic vinegar
75ml/5 tbsp olive oil
few drops of chilli sauce
4 canned artichoke hearts, drained and sliced
salt and ground black pepper
basil leaves, to garnish

SERVES 6

1. Preheat the oven to 200°C/400°F/Gas 6. Lightly oil a foil-lined baking sheet and place the whole peppers on the foil. Bake for about 45 minutes until beginning to char. Cover with a dish towel and leave to cool for 5 minutes.

2. Slice the sun-dried tomatoes into thin strips. Thinly slice the garlic. Set the tomatoes and garlic aside.

3. Beat together the vinegar, oil and chilli sauce, then season with a little salt and pepper.

4. Peel and slice the peppers. Mix with the artichokes, tomatoes and garlic. Pour over the dressing and scatter with the basil leaves.

FONDUTA

Fontina is an Italian medium-fat cheese with a rich salty flavour, a little like gruyère, which makes a good substitute. This delicious cheese dip needs only some warm ciabatta or focaccia, a herby salad and some robust red wine for a thoroughly enjoyable meal.

250g/9oz fontina cheese, diced
250ml/8fl oz/1 cup milk
15g/½oz /1 tbsp butter
2 eggs, lightly beaten
ground black pepper

SERVES 4

1 Put the cheese in a bowl with the milk and leave to soak for 2–3 hours. Transfer to a double boiler or a heatproof bowl set over a pan of simmering water.

2 Add the butter and eggs and cook gently, stirring until the cheese has melted to a smooth sauce with the consistency of custard.

3 Remove from the heat and season with pepper. Transfer to a serving dish and serve immediately.

COOK'S TIP
Don't overheat the sauce, or the eggs might curdle. A very gentle heat will produce a lovely smooth sauce.

GARLIC PRAWNS

For this simple Spanish tapas dish, you really need fresh raw prawns which absorb the flavours of the garlic and chilli as they fry. Have everything ready for last minute cooking so you can take it to the table still sizzling.

350–450g/12oz–1lb large
raw prawns
2 red chillies
75ml/5 tbsp olive oil
3 garlic cloves, crushed
salt and ground black pepper

SERVES 4

1 Remove the heads and shells from the prawns, leaving the tails intact.

2 Halve each chilli lengthways and discard the seeds. Heat the oil in a flameproof pan, suitable for serving. (Alternatively, use a frying pan and have a warmed serving dish ready in the oven.)

3 Add all the prawns, chilli and garlic to the pan and cook over a high heat for about 3 minutes, stirring until the prawns turn pink. Season lightly with salt and pepper and serve immediately.

CHORIZO IN OLIVE OIL

Spanish chorizo sausage has a deliciously pungent taste; its robust seasoning of garlic, chilli and paprika flavours the ingredients it is cooked with. Frying chorizo with onions and olive oil is one of its simplest and most delicious uses.

75ml/5 tbsp extra virgin olive oil
350g/12oz chorizo sausage, sliced
1 large onion, thinly sliced
roughly chopped flat leaf parsley,
to garnish

SERVES 4

1 Heat the oil in a frying pan and fry the chorizo sausage over a high heat until beginning to colour. Remove from pan with slotted spoon.

2 Add the onion to the pan and fry until coloured. Return the sausage slices to the pan and heat through for 1 minute.

3 Tip the mixture into a shallow serving dish and scatter with the parsley. Serve with warm bread.

VARIATION
Chorizo is usually available in large supermarkets or delicatessens. Other similarly rich, spicy sausages can be used as a substitute.

CROSTINI

These are Italian canapés, consisting of toasted slices of bread, spread with various toppings. The following recipes are for a chicken liver pâté and a prawn butter.

FOR THE CHICKEN LIVER PATE
150g/5oz/⅔ cup butter
1 small onion, finely chopped
1 garlic clove, crushed
225g/8oz chicken livers
4 sage leaves, chopped
salt and ground black pepper

FOR THE PRAWN BUTTER
225g/8oz cooked, peeled prawns
2 drained canned anchovies
115g/4oz/¼ cup butter, softened
15ml/1 tbsp lemon juice
15ml/1 tbsp chopped fresh parsley
salt and ground black pepper

FOR THE CROSTINI
12 slices crusty Italian or
French pain de campagne *bread, cut*
1cm/½ in thick
75g/3oz/6 tbsp butter, melted

FOR THE GARNISH
sage leaves
flat leaf parsley

SERVES 6

| 3 | Bake for 8–10 minutes, until pale golden. Spread half the hot crostini with the pâté and the rest with the prawn butter, garnishing with sage and parsley, respectively. Serve the crostini at once.

COOK'S TIP
Both the chicken liver pâté and the prawn butter can be made ahead, but should be used within two days. Cover both toppings closely and store them in the fridge.

| 1 | To make the chicken liver pâté, melt half the butter in a frying pan, add the onion and garlic, and fry gently until soft. Add the chicken livers and sage and sauté for about 8 minutes, until the livers are brown and firm. Season with salt and pepper and process in a blender or food processor with the remaining butter.

| 2 | To make the prawn butter, chop the prawns and anchovies finely. Place in a bowl with the butter and beat together until well blended. Add the lemon juice and parsley and season with salt and pepper. Preheat the oven to 200°C/400°F/Gas 6. Place the bread slices on one or two baking sheets and brush with the butter.

MARINATED BABY AUBERGINES WITH RAISINS AND PINE NUTS

Aubergines are popular in all the Mediterranean countries. This is a recipe with an Italian influence, using ingredients that have been included in recipes since Renaissance times. Make a day in advance, to allow the sour and sweet flavours to develop.

12 baby aubergines, halved
lengthways
250ml/8fl oz/1 cup extra virgin
olive oil
juice of 1 lemon
30ml/2 tbsp balsamic vinegar
3 cloves
25g/1oz/⅓ cup pine nuts
25g/1oz/2 tbsp raisins
15ml/1 tbsp granulated sugar
1 bay leaf
large pinch of dried chilli flakes
salt and ground black pepper

SERVES 4

1 Preheat the grill to high. Place the aubergines, cut side up, in the grill pan and brush with a little of the olive oil. Grill for 10 minutes, until slightly blackened, turning them over half way through cooking.

2 To make the marinade, put the remaining olive oil, the lemon juice, vinegar, cloves, pine nuts, raisins, sugar and bay leaf in a jug. Add the chilli flakes and salt and pepper and mix well.

3 Place the hot aubergines in an earthenware or glass bowl, and pour over the marinade. Leave to cool, turning the aubergines once or twice. Serve cold.

YOGURT CHEESE IN OLIVE OIL

Sheep's milk is widely used in cheese making in the Eastern Mediterranean, particularly in Greece where sheep's yogurt is hung in muslin to drain off the whey before patting into balls of soft cheese. Here it's bottled in olive oil with chilli and herbs — an appropriate gift for a "foodie" friend.

750g/1¾lb Greek sheep's yogurt
2.5ml/½ tsp salt
10ml/2 tsp crushed dried chillies or chilli powder
15ml/1 tbsp chopped fresh rosemary
15ml/1 tbsp chopped fresh thyme or oregano
about 300ml/½ pint/1¼ cups olive oil, preferably garlic-flavoured

FILLS TWO 450G/1LB JARS

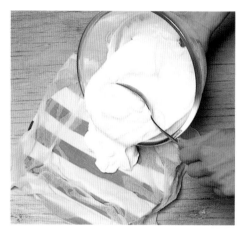

1 Sterilize a 30cm/12in square of muslin by steeping it in boiling water. Drain and lay over a large plate. Mix the yogurt with the salt and tip on to the centre of the muslin. Bring up the sides of the muslin and tie firmly with string.

2 Hang the bag on a kitchen cupboard handle or suitable position where the bag can be suspended with a bowl underneath to catch the whey. Leave for 2–3 days until the yogurt stops dripping.

3 Sterilize two 450g/1lb glass preserving or jam jars by heating them in the oven at 150°C/300°F/Gas 2 for 15 minutes.

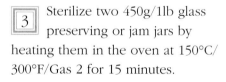

4 Mix together the chilli and herbs. Take teaspoonfuls of the cheese and roll into balls with your hands. Lower into the jars, sprinkling each layer with the herb mixture.

5   Pour the oil over the cheese until completely covered. Store in the fridge for up to 3 weeks.

6   To serve the cheese, spoon out of the jars with a little of the flavoured olive oil and spread on to lightly toasted bread.

COOK'S TIP
If your kitchen is particularly warm, find a cooler place to suspend the cheese. Alternatively, drain the cheese in the fridge, suspending the bag from one of the shelves.

TAPENADE AND HERB AÏOLI WITH SUMMER VEGETABLES

A beautiful platter of salad vegetables served with one or two interesting sauces makes a thoroughly appetizing and informal starter. This colourful French appetizer is perfect for entertaining as it can be prepared in advance.

FOR THE TAPENADE
175g/6oz/1½ cups pitted black olives
50g/2oz can anchovy fillets, drained
30ml/2 tbsp capers
120ml/4fl oz/½ cup olive oil
finely grated rind of 1 lemon
15ml/1 tbsp brandy (optional)
ground black pepper

FOR THE HERB AÏOLI
2 egg yolks
5ml/1 tsp Dijon mustard
10ml/2 tsp white wine vinegar
250ml/8fl oz/1 cup light olive oil
45ml/3 tbsp chopped mixed fresh herbs, such as chervil, parsley or tarragon
30ml/2 tbsp chopped watercress
5 garlic cloves, crushed
salt and ground black pepper

TO SERVE
2 red peppers, seeded and cut into wide strips
30ml/2 tbsp olive oil
225g/8oz new potatoes
115g/4oz green beans
225g/8oz baby carrots
225g/8oz young asparagus
12 quail's eggs (optional)
fresh herbs, to garnish
coarse salt for sprinkling

SERVES 6

1 To make the tapenade, finely chop the olives, anchovies and capers and beat together with the oil, lemon rind and brandy if using. (Alternatively, lightly process the ingredients in a blender or food processor, scraping down the mixture from the sides of the bowl if necessary.)

2 Season with pepper and blend in a little more oil if the mixture is very dry. Transfer to a serving dish.

3 To make the aïoli, beat together the egg yolks, mustard and vinegar. Gradually blend in the oil, a trickle at a time, whisking well after each addition until thick and smooth. Season with salt and pepper to taste, adding a little more vinegar if the aïoli tastes bland.

4 Stir in the mixed herbs, watercress and garlic, then transfer to a serving dish. Cover and put in the fridge.

5 Put the peppers on a foil-lined grill rack and brush with the oil. Grill under a high heat until just beginning to char.

6 Cook the potatoes in a large pan of boiling, salted water until just tender. Add the beans and carrots and cook for 1 minute. Add the asparagus and cook for a further 30 seconds. Drain the vegetables.

7 Cook the quail's eggs in boiling water for 2 minutes. Drain and remove half of each shell.

8 Arrange all the vegetables, eggs and sauces on a serving platter. Garnish with fresh herbs and serve with coarse salt for sprinkling.

COOK'S TIP
Keep any leftover sauces for serving with salads. The tapenade is also delicious tossed with pasta or spread on to warm toast.

GRILLED VEGETABLE TERRINE

A colourful, layered terrine, using all the vegetables associated with the Mediterranean.

2 large red peppers, quartered, cored
and seeded
2 large yellow peppers, quartered,
cored and seeded
1 large aubergine, sliced lengthways
2 large courgettes, sliced lengthways
90ml/6 tbsp olive oil
1 large red onion, thinly sliced
75g/3oz/½ cup raisins
15ml/1 tbsp tomato purée
15ml/1 tbsp red wine vinegar
400ml/14fl oz/1⅔ cups tomato juice
15g/½oz/2 tbsp powdered gelatine
fresh basil leaves, to garnish

FOR THE DRESSING
90ml/6 tbsp extra virgin olive oil
30ml/2 tbsp red wine vinegar
salt and ground black pepper

SERVES 6

2   Arrange the aubergine and courgette slices on separate baking sheets. Brush them with a little oil and cook under the grill, turning occasionally, until tender and golden.

3   Heat the remaining olive oil in a frying pan, and add the sliced onion, raisins, tomato purée and red wine vinegar. Cook gently until soft and syrupy. Leave to cool in the frying pan.

4   Line a 1.75 litre/3 pint/7½ cup terrine with clear film, (it helps to lightly oil the terrine first) leaving a little hanging over the sides.

5   Pour half the tomato juice into a saucepan, and sprinkle with the gelatine. Dissolve gently over a low heat, stirring.

6   Place a layer of red peppers in the bottom of the terrine, and pour in enough of the tomato juice with gelatine to cover. Continue layering the aubergine, courgettes, yellow peppers and onion mixture, finishing with another layer of red peppers. Pour tomato juice over each layer of vegetables.

7   Add the remaining tomato juice to any left in the pan, and pour into the terrine. Give it a sharp tap, to disperse the juice. Cover the terrine and chill until set.

8   To make the dressing, whisk together the oil and vinegar, and season. Turn out the terrine and remove the clear film. Serve in thick slices, drizzled with dressing. Garnish with basil leaves.

1   Place the prepared red and yellow peppers skin side up under a hot grill and cook until the skins are blackened. Transfer to a bowl and cover with a plate. Leave to cool.

SOUPS

Soups are a vital part of the culinary heritage of
the Mediterranean. From winter warmers to
summer coolers, there's a soup for every season.

LEFT: In Morocco the nights can be bitterly cold, and a bowl of hot, spicy soup is very welcome.

BELOW: In autumn, when Majorca's almond trees are heavy with the delicious nuts, farm workers spread nets on the ground and use long poles to knock them down. The reward for their labours is a delicately-flavoured soup.

Soups were, and still are, an important part of the Mediterranean diet. In the past, when a lot of the countries were poverty-stricken, soup constituted a meal for many. These broths were made with beans, lentils and other pulses, particularly during the cold winter months. Eaten with plenty of bread, they were filling and provided nourishment. Fresh vegetables were added in season, and sometimes eggs. Many of these soups, therefore, were extremely simple. Some of the recipes that exist today have been passed down through the generations, only to be given new life, and new status, with the rising popularity of "peasant food" in restaurants and cookbooks. These are unfussy recipes, which rely for their success on the quality of the ingredients. Take garlic soup, for example, which is made in various ways throughout Spain and France; in its simplest form, it is nothing but garlic, water and seasoning, but with the best garlic, these basic ingredients are transformed into a delicious and fragrant liquor. This basic method is applied to many vegetables, with the water sometimes replaced with a meat stock, and the mixture sometimes passed through a sieve, to produce a smooth soup.

Pumpkins, Jerusalem artichokes, tomatoes, peppers, asparagus and spinach are just a few of the many varieties of vegetables used to make soup.

Soups containing meat are usually hearty, combined as they are with pulses such as lentils, chick-peas, or potatoes, rice or pasta. In the Middle East, beef and lamb are used, and soups are seasoned with spices and herbs. There are special feast day soups, and soups to eat after sunset during the fast of Ramadan. However, the more typical Mediterranean soup is based on vegetables, pulses,

ABOVE: Dawn in Corfu, and a fisherman prepares to head out to sea.

and of course, fish and seafood. Wonderful fish soups come in numerous different guises; the now famous, and often poorly imitated *bouillabaisse* is a "stew" of various varieties of fish and seafood native to the coast of the south of France, and the port of Marseilles, where the dish originated. Again, these soups serve as complete meals, sometimes with the fish and broth offered separately, accompanied by bread or toasted croûtes.

Every country and coastal region has its own speciality, and often the soup will never be quite the same, the ingredients depending on the fishermen's catch that day. Many of the recipes were originated by the fishermen themselves, who cooked them on the boats, using the fish which they couldn't sell in the market, because it had no commercial value. Today, with a wide choice of fish available in fishmongers and supermarkets, it is pos-

sible to recreate many of these wonderful dishes at home.

Chilled soups come from the south of Spain, where *gazpacho* is extremely popular – this is a delicious and refreshing mixture of raw tomatoes, peppers and cucumbers which makes the perfect lunch for a hot summer day. Again, there are variations on this classic recipe, with such diverse ingredients as almonds and grapes. Cold soups also feature in the Middle East – these are yogurt-based, usually mixed with cucumber and garlic, spiked with mint.

Tourists who travel to the Mediterranean seldom sample more than a few of the many different soups on offer, but it is worth investigating that delicious smell wafting from a restaurant kitchen, or asking the name of that delectable-looking soup that is being enjoyed at the next table.

Changing at the whim of the cook, or to take best advantage of the finest market produce, Mediterranean soups are certainly a cause for celebration.

BOUILLABAISSE

Perhaps the most famous of all Mediterranean fish soups, this recipe, originating from Marseilles in the south of France, is a rich and colourful mixture of fish and shellfish, flavoured with tomatoes, saffron and orange.

1.5kg/3–3½lb mixed fish and raw shellfish, such as red mullet, John Dory, monkfish, red snapper, whiting, large prawns and clams
225g/8oz well-flavoured tomatoes
pinch of saffron strands
90ml/6 tbsp olive oil
1 onion, sliced
1 leek, sliced
1 celery stick, sliced
2 garlic cloves, crushed
1 bouquet garni
1 strip pared orange rind
2.5ml/½ tsp fennel seeds
salt and ground black pepper
15ml/1 tbsp tomato purée
10ml/2 tsp Pernod
4–6 thick slices French bread
45ml/3 tbsp chopped fresh parsley

SERVES 4–6

1   Remove the heads, tails and fins from the fish and put them in a large pan, with 1.2 litres/2 pints/5 cups water. Bring to the boil, and simmer for 15 minutes. Strain, and reserve the liquid.

2   Cut the fish into large chunks. Leave the shellfish in their shells. Scald the tomatoes, then drain and refresh in cold water. Peel and roughly chop them. Soak the saffron in 15–30ml/1–2 tbsp hot water.

3   Heat the oil in a large pan, add the onion, leek and celery and cook until softened. Add the garlic, bouquet garni, orange rind, fennel seeds and tomatoes, then stir in the saffron and liquid and the fish stock. Season with salt and pepper, then bring to the boil and simmer for 30–40 minutes.

4   Add the shellfish and boil for about 6 minutes. Add the fish and cook for a further 6–8 minutes, until it flakes easily.

5   Using a slotted spoon, transfer the fish to a warmed serving platter. Keep the liquid boiling, to allow the oil to emulsify with the broth. Add the tomato purée and Pernod, then check the seasoning. To serve, place a slice of French bread in each soup bowl, pour the broth over the top and serve the fish separately, sprinkled with the parsley.

CHILLED ALMOND SOUP

Unless you want to spend time pounding the ingredients for this dish by hand, a food processor is essential.
Then you'll find that this Spanish soup is very simple to make and refreshing to eat on a hot day.

115g/4oz fresh white bread
115g/4oz/1 cup blanched almonds
2 garlic cloves, sliced
75ml/5 tbsp olive oil
25ml/1½ tbsp sherry vinegar
salt and ground black pepper
toasted flaked almonds and
seedless green and black grapes,
halved and skinned, to garnish

SERVES 6

1   Break the bread into a bowl and pour over 150ml/¼ pint/ ⅔ cup cold water. Leave for 5 minutes.

2   Put the almonds and garlic in a blender or food processor and process until very finely ground. Blend in the soaked white bread.

3   Gradually add the oil until the mixture forms a smooth paste. Add the sherry vinegar then 600ml/ 1 pint/2½ cups cold water and process until smooth.

4   Transfer to a bowl and season with salt and pepper, adding a little more water if the soup is very thick. Chill for at least 2–3 hours.

5   Ladle the soup into bowls and scatter with the toasted almonds and skinned grapes.

GAZPACHO

There are many versions of this refreshingly chilled, pungent soup from southern Spain. All contain an intense blend of tomatoes, peppers, cucumber and garlic; perfect on a hot summer's evening.

900g/2lb ripe tomatoes
1 cucumber
2 red peppers, seeded and
roughly chopped
2 garlic cloves, crushed
175g/6oz/3 cups fresh white
breadcrumbs
30ml/2 tbsp white wine vinegar
30ml/2 tbsp sun-dried tomato paste
90ml/6 tbsp olive oil
salt and ground black pepper

To finish
1 slice white bread, crust removed
and cut into cubes
30ml/2 tbsp olive oil
6–12 ice cubes
small bowl of mixed chopped
garnishes, such as tomato, cucumber,
red onion, hard-boiled egg and flat
leaf parsley or tarragon leaves

Serves 6

COOK'S TIP
The sun-dried tomato paste has been added to accentuate the flavour of the tomatoes. You might not need this if you use a really flavoursome variety.

2 Process half the mixture in a blender or food processor until fairly smooth. Process the remaining mixture and mix with the first.

3 Check the seasoning and add a little cold water if the soup is too thick. Chill for several hours.

1 Plunge the tomatoes into boiling water for 30 seconds, then refresh in cold water. Peel away the skins and quarter. Peel and roughly chop the cucumber. Mix the tomatoes and cucumber in a bowl with the peppers, garlic, bread-crumbs, vinegar, tomato paste and olive oil and season lightly with salt and pepper.

4 To finish, fry the bread in the oil until golden. Spoon the soup into bowls, adding one or two ice cubes to each. Serve accompanied by the croûtons and garnishes.

SPICED MUSSEL SOUP

Chunky and colourful, this Turkish fish soup is like a chowder in its consistency. It's flavoured with harissa sauce, more familiar in North African cookery.

1.5kg/3–3½lb fresh mussels
150ml/¼ pint/⅔ cup white wine
3 tomatoes
30ml/2 tbsp olive oil
1 onion, finely chopped
2 garlic cloves, crushed
2 celery sticks, thinly sliced
bunch of spring onions, thinly sliced
1 potato, diced
7.5ml/1½ tsp harissa sauce
45ml/3 tbsp chopped fresh parsley
ground black pepper
thick yogurt, to serve (optional)

SERVES 6

1 Scrub the mussels, discarding any damaged ones or any open ones that do not close when tapped with a knife.

2 Bring the wine to the boil in a large saucepan. Add the mussels and cover with a lid. Cook for 4–5 minutes until the mussels have opened wide. Discard any mussels that remain closed. Drain the mussels, reserving the cooking liquid. Reserve a few mussels in their shells for garnish and shell the rest.

3 Peel the tomatoes and dice them. Heat the oil in a pan and fry the onion, garlic, celery and spring onions for 5 minutes.

4 Add the shelled mussels, reserved liquid, potato, harissa sauce and tomatoes. Bring just to the boil, reduce the heat and cover. Simmer gently for 25 minutes, or until the potatoes are breaking up.

5 Stir in the parsley and pepper and add the reserved mussels. Heat through for 1 minute. Serve hot with a spoonful of yogurt, if you like.

GREEN LENTIL SOUP

Lentil soup is an Eastern Mediterranean classic, varying in its spiciness according to region. Red or puy lentils make an equally good substitute for the green lentils used here.

225g/8oz/1 cup green lentils
75ml/5 tbsp olive oil
3 onions, finely chopped
2 garlic cloves, thinly sliced
10ml/2 tsp cumin seeds, crushed
1.5ml/¼ tsp ground turmeric
600ml/1 pint/2½ cups chicken or
vegetable stock
salt and ground black pepper
30ml/2 tbsp roughly chopped
fresh coriander, to finish

SERVES 4–6

1 Put the lentils in a saucepan and cover with cold water. Bring to the boil and boil rapidly for 10 minutes. Drain.

2 Heat 30ml/2 tbsp of the oil in a pan and fry two of the onions with the garlic, cumin and turmeric for 3 minutes, stirring. Add the lentils, stock and 600ml/1 pint/2½ cups water. Bring to the boil, reduce the heat, cover and simmer gently for 30 minutes, until the lentils are soft.

3 Fry the third onion in the remaining oil until golden.

4 Use a potato masher to lightly mash the lentils and make the soup pulpy. Reheat gently and season with salt and pepper to taste. Pour the soup into bowls. Stir the fresh coriander into the fried onion and scatter over the soup. Serve with warm bread.

MOROCCAN HARIRA

This is a hearty meat and vegetable soup, eaten during the month of Ramadan, when the Muslim population fast between sunrise and sunset.

450g/1lb well-flavoured tomatoes
225g/8oz lamb, cut into 1cm/½in pieces
2.5ml/½ tsp ground turmeric
2.5ml/½ tsp ground cinnamon
25g/1oz/2 tbsp butter
60ml/4 tbsp chopped fresh coriander
30ml/2 tbsp chopped fresh parsley
1 onion, chopped
50g/2oz/¼ cup split red lentils
75g/3oz/½ cup dried chick-peas, soaked overnight
4 baby onions or small shallots, peeled
25g/1oz/¼ cup soup noodles
salt and ground black pepper
chopped fresh coriander, lemon slices and ground cinnamon, to garnish

SERVES 4

1 Plunge the tomatoes into boiling water for 30 seconds, then refresh in cold water. Peel away the skins. Cut into quarters and remove the seeds. Chop roughly.

2 Put the lamb, turmeric, cinnamon, butter, coriander, parsley and onion into a large pan, and cook over a moderate heat, stirring, for 5 minutes. Add the chopped tomatoes and continue to cook for 10 minutes.

3 Rinse the lentils under running water and add to the pan with the drained chick-peas and 600ml/1 pint/2½ cups water. Season with salt and pepper. Bring to the boil, cover, and simmer gently for 1½ hours.

4 Add the baby onions and cook for a further 30 minutes. Add the noodles 5 minutes before the end of this cooking time. Garnish with the coriander, lemon slices and cinnamon.

RIBOLLITA

Ribollita is rather like minestrone, but includes beans instead of pasta. In Italy it is traditionally served ladled over bread and a rich green vegetable, although you could omit this for a lighter version.

45ml/3 tbsp olive oil
2 onions, chopped
2 carrots, sliced
4 garlic cloves, crushed
2 celery sticks, thinly sliced
1 fennel bulb, trimmed and chopped
2 large courgettes, thinly sliced
400g/14oz can chopped tomatoes
30ml/2 tbsp home-made or bought pesto
900ml/1½ pints/3¾ cups vegetable stock
400g/14oz can haricot or borlotti beans, drained
salt and ground black pepper

To Finish
450g/1lb young spinach
15ml/1 tbsp extra virgin olive oil, plus extra for drizzling
6–8 slices white bread
Parmesan cheese shavings

Serves 6–8

Variation
Use other dark greens, such as chard or cabbage instead of the spinach; shred and cook until tender.

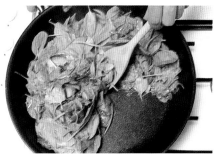

1 Heat the oil in a large saucepan. Add the onions, carrots, garlic, celery and fennel and fry gently for 10 minutes. Add the courgettes and fry for a further 2 minutes.

2 Add the chopped tomatoes, pesto, stock and beans and bring to the boil. Reduce the heat, cover and simmer gently for 25–30 minutes, until the vegetables are completely tender. Season with salt and pepper to taste.

3 To serve, fry the spinach in the oil for 2 minutes or until wilted. Spoon over the bread in soup bowls, then ladle the soup over the spinach. Serve with extra olive oil for drizzling on to the soup and Parmesan cheese to sprinkle on top.

SEAFOOD SOUP WITH ROUILLE

This is a really chunky, aromatic mixed fish soup from France, flavoured with plenty of saffron and herbs. Rouille, a fiery hot paste, is served separately for everyone to swirl into their soup to flavour.

3 gurnard or red mullet, scaled and gutted
12 large prawns
675g/1½ lb white fish, such as cod, haddock, halibut or monkfish
225g/8oz fresh mussels
1 onion, quartered
5ml/1 tsp saffron strands
75ml/5 tbsp olive oil
1 fennel bulb, roughly chopped
4 garlic cloves, crushed
3 strips pared orange rind
4 thyme sprigs
675g/1½lb tomatoes or 400g/14oz can chopped tomatoes
30ml/2 tbsp sun-dried tomato paste
3 bay leaves
salt and ground black pepper

FOR THE ROUILLE
1 red pepper, seeded and roughly chopped
1 red chilli, seeded and sliced
2 garlic cloves, chopped
75ml/5 tbsp olive oil
15g/½oz/¼ cup fresh breadcrumbs

SERVES 6

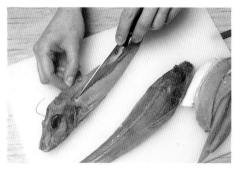

2 Fillet the gurnard or mullet by cutting away the flesh from either side of the backbone, reserving the heads and bones. Cut the fillets into small chunks. Shell half the prawns and reserve the trimmings to make the stock. Skin the white fish, discarding any bones, and cut into large chunks. Scrub the mussels well, discarding any damaged ones or any open ones that do not close when tapped sharply with the back of a knife.

3 Put the fish trimmings and prawn trimmings in a saucepan with the onion and 1.2 litres/2 pints/5 cups water. Bring to the boil, then simmer gently for 30 minutes. Cool slightly and strain.

4 Soak the saffron in 15ml/1 tbsp boiling water. Heat 30ml/2 tbsp of the oil in a large sauté pan or saucepan. Add the gurnard or mullet and white fish and fry over a high heat for 1 minute. Drain.

5 Heat the remaining oil and fry the fennel, garlic, orange rind and thyme until beginning to colour. Make up the strained stock to about 1.2 litres/2 pints/5 cups with water.

1 To make the rouille, process the pepper, chilli, garlic, oil and breadcrumbs in a blender or food processor until smooth. Transfer to a serving dish and chill.

COOK'S TIP
To save time, order the fish and ask the fishmonger to fillet the gurnard or mullet for you.

6 If using fresh tomatoes, plunge them into boiling water for 30 seconds, then refresh in cold water. Peel and chop. Add the stock to the pan with the saffron, tomatoes, tomato paste and bay leaves. Season, bring almost to the boil, then simmer gently, covered, for 20 minutes.

7 Stir in the gurnard or mullet, white fish and prawns and add the mussels. Cover the pan and cook for 3–4 minutes. Discard any mussels that do not open. Serve the soup hot with the rouille.

SPICY PUMPKIN SOUP

—

*Pumpkin is popular all over the Mediterranean and it's an important ingredient in Middle Eastern
cookery, from which this soup is inspired. Ginger and cumin give the soup its spicy flavour.*

900g/2lb pumpkin, peeled and
seeds removed
30ml/2 tbsp olive oil
2 leeks, trimmed and sliced
1 garlic clove, crushed
5ml/1 tsp ground ginger
5ml/1 tsp ground cumin
900ml/1½ pints/3¾ cups chicken stock
salt and ground black pepper
coriander leaves, to garnish
60ml/4 tbsp natural yogurt, to serve

SERVES 4

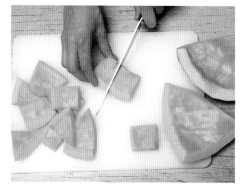

☐1 Cut the pumpkin into chunks.
Heat the oil in a large pan and
add the leeks and garlic. Cook gently
until softened.

☐2 Add the ginger and cumin and
cook, stirring, for a further
minute. Add the pumpkin and the
chicken stock and season with salt
and pepper. Bring to the boil and
simmer for 30 minutes, until the
pumpkin is tender. Process the soup,
in batches if necessary, in a blender
or food processor.

☐3 Reheat the soup and serve in
warmed individual bowls, with
a swirl of yogurt and a garnish of
coriander leaves.

MIDDLE EASTERN YOGURT AND CUCUMBER SOUP

Yogurt is used extensively in Middle Eastern cookery, and it is usually made at home. Sometimes it is added at the end of cooking a dish, to prevent it from curdling, but in this cold soup the yogurt is one of the basic ingredients.

1 large cucumber, peeled
300ml/½ pint/1¼ cups single cream
150ml/¼ pint/⅔ cup natural yogurt
2 garlic cloves, crushed
30ml/2 tbsp white wine vinegar
15ml/1 tbsp chopped fresh mint
salt and ground black pepper
sprigs of mint, to garnish

SERVES 4

1 Grate the cucumber coarsely. Place in a bowl with the cream, yogurt, garlic, vinegar and mint. Stir well and season to taste.

2 Chill for at least 2 hours before serving. Just before serving, stir the soup again. Pour into individual bowls and garnish with mint sprigs.

PISTOU

A delicious vegetable soup from Nice in the south of France, served with a sun-dried tomato pesto, and fresh Parmesan cheese.

1 courgette, diced
1 small potato, diced
1 shallot, chopped
1 carrot, diced
225g/8oz can chopped tomatoes
1.2 litres/2 pints/5 cups vegetable stock
50g/2oz French beans, cut into
1cm/½in lengths
50g/2oz/½ cup frozen petits pois
50g/2oz/½ cup small pasta shapes
60–90ml/4–6 tbsp home-made or
bought pesto
15ml/1 tbsp sun-dried tomato paste
salt and ground black pepper
freshly grated Parmesan cheese,
to serve

SERVES 4–6

1 Place the courgette, potato, shallot, carrot and tomatoes in a large pan. Add the vegetable stock and season with salt and pepper. Bring to the boil, then cover and simmer for 20 minutes.

2 Add the French beans, petits pois and pasta. Cook for a further 10 minutes, until the pasta is tender. Adjust the seasoning.

3 Ladle the soup into individual bowls. Mix together the pesto and sun-dried tomato paste, and stir a spoonful into each serving. Serve with grated Parmesan cheese to sprinkle into each bowl.

AVGOLEMONO

This is the most popular of Greek soups. The name means egg and lemon, the two important ingredients,
which produce a light, nourishing soup. Orzo is Greek, rice-shaped pasta, but you can use any small shape.

1.75 litres/3 pints/7½ cups
chicken stock
115g/4oz/½ cup orzo pasta
3 eggs
juice of 1 large lemon
salt and ground black pepper
lemon slices, to garnish

SERVES 4–6

1 Pour the stock into a large pan, and bring to the boil. Add the pasta and cook for 5 minutes.

2 Beat the eggs until frothy, then add the lemon juice and a tablespoon of cold water. Slowly stir in a ladleful of the hot chicken stock, then add one or two more. Return this mixture to the pan, off the heat and stir well. Season with salt and pepper and serve at once, garnished with lemon slices. (Do not let the soup boil once the eggs have been added or it will curdle.)

GALICIAN BROTH

This delicious main meal soup is very similar to the warming, chunky meat and potato broths of cooler climates. For extra colour, a few onion skins can be added when cooking the gammon, but remember to remove them before serving.

450g/1lb gammon, in one piece
2 bay leaves
2 onions, sliced
10ml/2 tsp paprika
675g/1½lb potatoes, cut into
large chunks
225g/8oz spring greens
425g/15oz can haricot or cannellini
beans, drained
salt and ground black pepper

SERVES 4

2   Bring to the boil then reduce the heat and simmer very gently for about 1½ hours until the meat is tender. Keep an eye on the pan to make sure it doesn't boil over.

4   Cut away the cores from the greens. Roll up the leaves and cut into thin shreds. Add to the pan with the beans and simmer for about 10 minutes. Season with salt and pepper to taste and serve hot.

1   Soak the gammon overnight in cold water. Drain and put in a large saucepan with the bay leaves and onions. Pour over 1.5 litres/ 2½ pints/6¼ cups cold water.

3   Drain the meat, reserving the cooking liquid and leave to cool slightly. Discard the skin and any excess fat from the meat and cut into small chunks. Return to the pan with the paprika and potatoes. Cover and simmer gently for 20 minutes.

COOK'S TIP
Bacon knuckles can be used instead of the gammon. The bones will give the juices a delicious flavour.

FRESH TOMATO SOUP

Intensely flavoured sun-ripened tomatoes need little embellishment in this fresh-tasting soup. If you buy from the supermarket, choose the ripest looking ones and add the amount of sugar and vinegar necessary, depending on their natural sweetness. On a hot day this Italian soup is also delicious chilled.

1.5kg/3–3½lb ripe tomatoes
400ml/14fl oz/1⅔ cups chicken or
vegetable stock
45ml/3 tbsp sun-dried tomato paste
30–45ml/2–3 tbsp balsamic vinegar
10–15ml/2–3 tsp caster sugar
small handful basil leaves
salt and ground black pepper
basil leaves, to garnish
toasted cheese croûtes and
crème fraîche, to serve

SERVES 6

1 Plunge the tomatoes into boiling water for 30 seconds, then refresh in cold water. Peel away the skins and quarter the tomatoes. Put them in a large saucepan and pour over the chicken or vegetable stock. Bring just to the boil, reduce the heat, cover and simmer gently for 10 minutes until the tomatoes are pulpy.

2 Stir in the tomato paste, vinegar, sugar and basil. Season with salt and pepper, then cook gently, stirring, for 2 minutes. Process the soup in a blender or food processor, then return to the pan and reheat gently. Serve in bowls topped with one or two toasted cheese croûtes and a spoonful of crème fraîche, garnished with basil leaves.

ED TOMATO AND SWEET PEPPER SOUP

*spired by the Spanish gazpacho, the difference being that this soup is cooked first,
and then chilled.*

2 red peppers, halved, cored
and seeded
45ml/3 tbsp olive oil
1 onion, finely chopped
2 garlic cloves, crushed
675g/1½ lb ripe well-flavoured
tomatoes
150ml/¼ pint/⅔ cup red wine
600ml/1 pint/2½ cups chicken stock
salt and ground black pepper
snipped fresh chives, to garnish

FOR THE CROUTONS
2 slices white bread, crusts removed
60ml/4 tbsp olive oil

SERVES 4

1 Cut each pepper half into quarters. Place skin side up on a grill rack and cook until the skins have charred. Transfer to a bowl and cover with a plate.

2 Heat the oil in a large pan. Add the onion and garlic and cook until soft. Meanwhile, remove the skin from the peppers and roughly chop them. Cut the tomatoes into chunks.

3 Add the peppers and tomatoes to the pan, then cover and cook gently for 10 minutes. Add the wine and cook for a further 5 minutes, then add the stock and salt and pepper and continue to simmer for 20 minutes.

4 To make the croûtons, cut the bread into cubes. Heat the oil in a small frying pan, add the bread and fry until golden. Drain on kitchen paper and store in an airtight box.

5 Process the soup in a blender or food processor until smooth. Pour into a clean glass or ceramic bowl and leave to cool thoroughly before chilling in the fridge for at least 3 hours. When the soup is cold, season to taste.

6 Serve the soup in bowls, topped with the croûtons and garnished with snipped chives.

SPANISH GARLIC SOUP

This is a simple and satisfying soup, made with one of the most popular ingredients in the Mediterranean — garlic!

30ml/2 tbsp olive oil
4 large garlic cloves, peeled
4 slices French bread, 5mm/¼in thick
15ml/1 tbsp paprika
1 litre/1¾ pints/4 cups beef stock
1.5ml/¼ tsp ground cumin
pinch of saffron strands
4 eggs
salt and ground black pepper
chopped fresh parsley, to garnish

SERVES 4

1 Preheat the oven to 230°C/ 450°F/Gas 8. Heat the oil in a large pan. Add the whole garlic cloves and cook until golden. Remove and set aside. Fry the bread in the oil until golden, then set aside.

2 Add the paprika to the pan, and fry for a few seconds. Stir in the beef stock, cumin and saffron, then add the reserved garlic, crushing the cloves with the back of a wooden spoon. Season with salt and pepper then cook for about 5 minutes.

3 Ladle the soup into four ovenproof bowls and break an egg into each. Place the slices of fried bread on top of the egg and place in the oven for about 3–4 minutes, until the eggs are set. Sprinkle with parsley and serve at once.

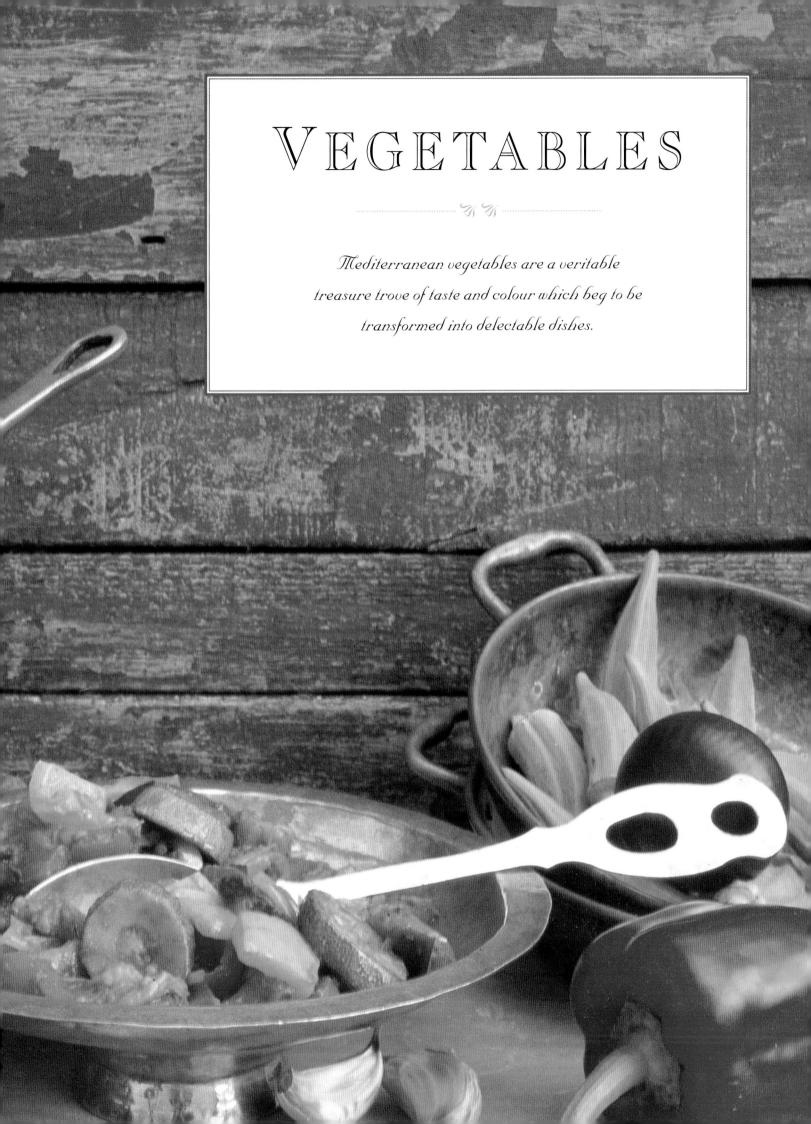

VEGETABLES

*Mediterranean vegetables are a veritable
treasure trove of taste and colour which beg to be
transformed into delectable dishes.*

A Mediterranean street market is a fascinating vision of colour and photo opportunities. The wonderful array of fruit and vegetable stalls in particular gives many "foodie" holiday-makers the urge to swap their hotel room for a kitchen in which to cook a feast of sweet, juicy local produce. Mediterranean vegetables have an inviting irregularity about them. Uneven colourings, knobbly skins and unsymmetrical shapes are a sure indication that the flesh inside will be full of flavour, a far cry from the mass-produced, artificially grown produce of colder climes. The dishes cooked using them are a joy to eat and even the simplest tossed salad of tomatoes and leaves, sprinkled with olive oil and seasoning, is worthy of serving solo — a meal in itself.

All around the Mediterranean, vegetables are the basis of everyday meals. This is due both to the cost of meat and to the religious obligations of fasting before festive occasions. This austerity has led to the development of many imaginative cookery skills. Deep fried, roasted, baked, stuffed, marinated, grilled, steamed; mixed in pies, tarts, omelettes, stews and stuffings; vegetables are very versatile.

BELOW: At a finca – or farm – in Andalusia, vegetables grow alongside grape-drying beds.

RIGHT: Tomatoes, chillies, potatoes and strings of garlic are just some of the vegetables on sale at this market in southern Turkey.

BELOW: The golden harvest: pumpkins make marvellous soups, pies and vegetable bakes.

In France and Italy vegetable fritters of courgette or aubergine, deep fried in a light crisp batter make a very enjoyable dish, often served with a ripe tomato sauce or garlicky herb dressing. Even the flowers of courgettes and marrows are battered and fried, making a visual and interesting garnish. Ratatouille, a wonderful stew of lightly cooked vegetables, is traditionally French, although similar recipes stretch right across the Mediterranean.

No vegetable is considered too small to bother with, while salad "thinnings" are included in mixed leafy salads, the smallest artichokes, turnips, aubergines and broad beans are put to good use in many dishes.

A stunning variety of mushrooms features highly in Italian and French cookery. In these countries markets are filled with wild varieties in the spring and autumn. The lovely shapes and flavours make interesting risottos and salads and may even be used to flavour pasta. Many mushroom varieties are dried for year-round availability. A small quantity goes a long way and can be used to enliven the flavour of everyday farmed mushrooms.

Stuffed vegetables are greatly loved in many countries of the Mediterranean, particularly in Turkey, Greece and the Middle East. Tomatoes, aubergines, peppers, courgettes and onions are filled with couscous, rice, herbs, spices, dried fruits, nuts, cheese and sometimes meat. Large leaves like spinach, vine and cabbage are stuffed with interesting ingredients, packed in a pan and gently cooked so as to mingle all the flavours together.

Even the humble potato takes pride of place at the Mediterranean table. The Spanish make a delicious potato salad in which new potatoes are fried to give a crisp crust. Italian gnocchi is a distinctively shaped, puréed and poached potato dish flavoured with a variety of herbs, cheese or mild spices.

MARINATED MUSHROOMS

This Spanish recipe makes a nice change from the French classic, mushrooms à la Grecque. Make this dish the day before you eat it, the flavour will improve with keeping.

30ml/2 tbsp olive oil
1 small onion, very finely chopped
1 garlic clove, crushed
15ml/1 tbsp tomato purée
50ml/2fl oz/¼ cup dry white wine
2 cloves
pinch of saffron strands
225g/8oz button mushrooms, trimmed
salt and ground black pepper
chopped fresh parsley, to garnish

SERVES 4

1 Heat the oil in a pan. Add the onion and garlic and cook until soft. Stir in the tomato purée, wine, 50ml/2fl oz/¼ cup water, cloves and saffron and season with salt and pepper. Bring to the boil, cover and simmer gently for 45 minutes, adding more water if it becomes too dry.

2 Add the mushrooms to the pan, then cover and simmer for a further 5 minutes. Remove from the heat and, still covered, allow to cool. Chill in the fridge overnight. Serve cold, sprinkled with chopped parsley.

POTATO AND ONION TORTILLA

One of the signature dishes of Spain, this delicious thick potato and onion omelette is eaten at all times of the day, hot or cold.

300ml/½ pint/1¼ cups olive oil
6 large potatoes, peeled and sliced
2 Spanish onions, sliced
6 size 2 eggs
salt and ground black pepper
cherry tomatoes, halved, to serve

SERVES 4

1 Heat the oil in a large non-stick frying pan. Stir in the potato, onion and a little salt. Cover and cook gently for 20 minutes until soft.

2 Beat the eggs in a large bowl. Remove the onion and potato from the pan with a slotted spoon and add to the eggs. Season with salt and pepper to taste. Pour off some of the oil, leaving about 60ml/4 tbsp in the pan. (Reserve the leftover oil for other cooking.) Heat the pan again.

3 When the oil is very hot, pour in the egg mixture. Cook for 2–3 minutes. Cover the pan with a plate and invert the omelette on to it. Slide it back into the pan and cook for a further 5 minutes, until golden brown and moist in the middle. Serve in wedges, with the tomatoes.

GRILLED AUBERGINE PARCELS

These are delicious little Italian bundles of tomatoes, mozzarella cheese and basil, wrapped in slices of aubergine.

2 large, long aubergines
225g/8oz mozzarella cheese
2 plum tomatoes
16 large basil leaves
salt and ground black pepper
30ml/2 tbsp olive oil

FOR THE DRESSING
60ml/4 tbsp olive oil
5ml/1 tsp balsamic vinegar
15ml/1 tbsp sun-dried tomato paste
15ml/1 tbsp lemon juice

FOR THE GARNISH
30ml/2 tbsp toasted pine nuts
torn basil leaves

SERVES 4

1 Remove the stalks from the aubergines and cut the aubergines lengthways into thin slices – the aim is to get 16 slices in total, disregarding the first and last slices (each about 5mm/¼in thick). (If you have a mandolin, it will cut perfect, even slices for you, otherwise, use a long-bladed, sharp knife.)

2 Bring a large pan of salted water to the boil and cook the aubergine slices for about 2 minutes, until just softened. Drain the sliced aubergines, then dry on kitchen paper.

3 Cut the mozzarella cheese into eight slices. Cut each tomato into eight slices, not counting the first and last slices.

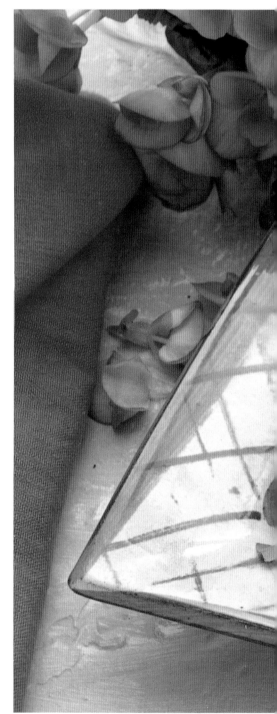

4 Take two aubergine slices and place on a flameproof tray or dish, in a cross (*left*). Place a slice of tomato in the centre, season with salt and pepper, then add a basil leaf, followed by a slice of mozzarella, another basil leaf, a slice of tomato and more seasoning.

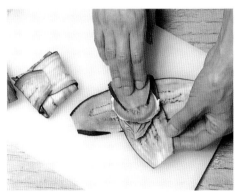

5 Fold the ends of the aubergine slices around the mozzarella and tomato filling to make a neat parcel (*left*). Repeat with the rest of the assembled ingredients to make eight parcels. Chill the parcels for about 20 minutes.

6 To make the tomato dressing, whisk together the olive oil, vinegar, sun-dried tomato paste and lemon juice. Season to taste.

7 Preheat the grill. Brush the parcels with olive oil and cook for about 5 minutes on each side, until golden. Serve hot, with the dressing, sprinkled with pine nuts and basil.

SPINACH AND RICOTTA GNOCCHI

The success of this Italian dish lies in not overworking the mixture, to achieve delicious, light mouthfuls.

900g/2lb fresh spinach
350g/12oz/1½ cups ricotta cheese
60ml/4 tbsp freshly grated
Parmesan cheese
3 size 2 eggs, beaten
1.5ml/¼ tsp grated nutmeg
45–60ml/3–4 tbsp plain flour
115g/4oz/½ cup butter, melted
salt and ground black pepper
freshly grated Parmesan cheese,
to serve

SERVES 4

 Place the spinach in a large pan and cook for 5 minutes, until wilted. Leave to cool, then squeeze the spinach as dry as possible. Process in a blender or food processor, then transfer to a bowl.

2 Add the ricotta, Parmesan, eggs and nutmeg. Season with salt and pepper and mix together. Add enough flour to make the mixture into a soft dough. Using your hands, shape the mixture into 7.5cm/3in sausages, then dust lightly with flour.

3 Bring a large pan of salted water to the boil. Gently slide the gnocchi into the water and cook for 1–2 minutes, until they float to the surface. Remove the gnocchi with a slotted spoon and transfer to a warmed dish. Pour over the melted butter and sprinkle with Parmesan cheese. Serve at once.

POLPETTES

Delicious little fried morsels of potato and Greek feta cheese, flavoured with dill and lemon juice.

500g/1¼lb potatoes
115g/4oz feta cheese
4 spring onions, chopped
45ml/3 tbsp chopped fresh dill
1 egg, beaten
15ml/1 tbsp lemon juice
salt and ground black pepper
flour for dredging
45ml/3 tbsp olive oil

SERVES 4

1 Boil the potatoes in their skins in lightly salted water until soft. Drain, then peel while still warm. Place in a bowl and mash. Crumble the feta cheese into the potatoes and add the spring onions, dill, egg and lemon juice and season with salt and pepper. (The cheese is salty, so taste before you add salt.) Stir well.

2 Cover the mixture and chill until firm. Divide the mixture into walnut-size balls, then flatten them slightly. Dredge with flour. Heat the oil in a frying pan and fry the polpettes until golden brown on each side. Drain on kitchen paper and serve at once.

STUFFED TOMATOES AND PEPPERS

Colourful peppers and tomatoes make perfect containers for various meat and vegetable stuffings. This rice and herb version uses typically Greek ingredients.

VARIATION

Small aubergines or large courgettes also make good vegetables for stuffing. Halve and scoop out the centres of the vegetables, then oil the vegetable cases and bake for about 15 minutes. Chop the centres, fry for 2–3 minutes to soften and add to the stuffing mixture. Fill the aubergine or courgette cases with the stuffing and bake as for the peppers and tomatoes.

2 large ripe tomatoes
1 green pepper
1 yellow or orange pepper
60ml/4 tbsp olive oil, plus extra
for sprinkling
2 onions, chopped
2 garlic cloves, crushed
50g/2oz/½ cup blanched
almonds, chopped
75g/3oz/scant ½ cup long grain rice,
boiled and drained
15g/½oz mint, roughly chopped
15g/½oz parsley, roughly chopped
25g/1oz/2 tbsp sultanas
45ml/3 tbsp ground almonds
salt and ground black pepper
chopped mixed herbs, to garnish

SERVES 4

1 Preheat the oven to 190°C/375°F/Gas 5. Cut the tomatoes in half and scoop out the pulp and seeds using a teaspoon. Leave the tomatoes to drain on kitchen paper with cut sides down. Roughly chop the tomato pulp and seeds.

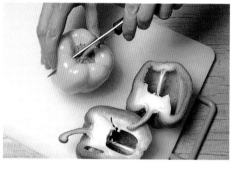

2 Halve the peppers, leaving the cores intact. Scoop out the seeds. Brush the peppers with 15ml/1 tbsp of the oil and bake on a baking tray for 15 minutes. Place the peppers and tomatoes in a shallow ovenproof dish and season with salt and pepper.

3 Fry the onions in the remaining oil for 5 minutes. Add the garlic and chopped almonds and fry for a further minute.

4 Remove the pan from the heat and stir in the rice, chopped tomatoes, mint, parsley and sultanas. Season well with salt and pepper and spoon the mixture into the tomatoes and peppers.

5 Pour 150ml/¼ pint/⅔ cup boiling water around the tomatoes and peppers and bake, uncovered, for 20 minutes. Scatter with the ground almonds and sprinkle with a little extra olive oil. Return to the oven and bake for a further 20 minutes, or until turning golden. Serve garnished with fresh herbs.

OKRA WITH CORIANDER AND TOMATOES

Okra is frequently combined with tomatoes and mild spices in various parts of the Mediterranean. Buy okra only if it is soft and velvety, not dry and shrivelled.

450g/1lb tomatoes or 400g/14oz can chopped tomatoes
450g/1lb fresh okra
45ml/3 tbsp olive oil
2 onions, thinly sliced
10ml/2 tsp coriander seeds, crushed
3 garlic cloves, crushed
2.5ml/½ tsp caster sugar
finely grated rind and juice of 1 lemon
salt and ground black pepper

SERVES 4

1   If using fresh tomatoes, plunge them into boiling water for 30 seconds, then refresh in cold water. Peel away the skins and chop.

2   Trim off any stalks from the okra and leave whole. Heat the oil in a sauté pan and fry the onions and coriander for 3–4 minutes until beginning to colour.

3   Add the okra and garlic and fry for 1 minute. Gently stir in the tomatoes and sugar and simmer gently for about 20 minutes, until the okra is tender, stirring once or twice. Stir in the lemon rind and juice and add salt and pepper to taste, adding a little more sugar if necessary. Serve warm or cold.

STUFFED PEPPERS

Couscous is a form of semolina, and is used extensively in the Middle East. It makes a good basis for a stuffing, combined with other ingredients.

6 peppers
25g/1oz/2 tbsp butter
1 onion, finely chopped
5ml/1 tsp olive oil
2.5ml/½ tsp salt
175g/6oz/1 cup couscous
25g/1oz/2 tbsp raisins
30ml/2 tbsp chopped fresh mint
1 egg yolk
salt and ground black pepper
mint leaves, to garnish

SERVES 4

1 Preheat the oven to 200°C/ 400°F/Gas 6. Carefully slit each pepper and remove the core and seeds. Melt the butter in a small pan and add the onion. Cook until soft.

2 To cook the couscous, bring 250ml/8fl oz/1 cup water to the boil. Add the oil and the salt, then remove the pan from the heat and add the couscous. Stir and leave to stand, covered, for 5 minutes. Stir in the cooked onion, raisins and mint, then season well with salt and pepper. Stir in the egg yolk.

3 Using a teaspoon, fill the peppers with the couscous mixture to only about three-quarters full, as the couscous will swell when cooked further. Place in a lightly oiled ovenproof dish and bake, uncovered, for about 20 minutes until tender. Serve hot or cold, garnished with the mint leaves.

COURGETTE FRITTERS WITH PISTOU

These delicious fritters are a speciality of Southern France. The pistou sauce provides a lovely contrast in flavour, but you could substitute other sauces, like a garlicky tomato one or a herb dressing.

FOR THE PISTOU
15g/½oz basil leaves
4 garlic cloves, crushed
90g/3½oz/1 cup grated
Parmesan cheese
finely grated rind of 1 lemon
150ml/¼ pint/⅔ cup olive oil

FOR THE FRITTERS
450g/1lb courgettes, grated
75g/3oz/⅔ cup plain flour
1 egg, separated
15ml/1 tbsp olive oil
oil for shallow frying
salt and ground black pepper

SERVES 4

1 To make the pistou, crush the basil leaves and garlic with a pestle and mortar to make a fairly fine paste. Transfer the paste to a bowl and stir in the grated cheese and lemon rind. Gradually blend in the oil, a little at a time, until combined, then transfer to a small serving dish.

2 To make the fritters, put the grated courgettes in a sieve over a bowl and sprinkle with plenty of salt. Leave for 1 hour then rinse thoroughly. Dry well on kitchen paper.

3 Sift the flour into a bowl and make a well in the centre, then add the egg yolk and oil. Measure 75ml/5 tbsp water and add a little to the bowl.

4 Whisk the egg yolk and oil, gradually incorporating the flour and water to make a smooth batter. Season and leave for 30 minutes.

5 Stir the courgettes into the batter. Whisk the egg white until stiff, then fold into the batter.

6 Heat 1cm/½in of oil in a frying pan. Add dessertspoons of batter to the oil and fry for 2 minutes until golden. Drain the fritters on kitchen paper and keep warm while frying the rest. Serve with the sauce.

RATATOUILLE

A highly versatile vegetable stew from Provence. Ratatouille is delicious hot or cold, on its own or with eggs, pasta, fish or meat — particularly roast lamb.

900g/2lb ripe, well-flavoured tomatoes
120ml/4fl oz/½ cup olive oil
2 onions, thinly sliced
2 red peppers, seeded and cut into chunks
1 yellow or orange pepper, seeded and cut into chunks
1 large aubergine, cut into chunks
2 courgettes, cut into thick slices
4 garlic cloves, crushed
2 bay leaves
15ml/1 tbsp chopped young thyme
salt and ground black pepper

SERVES 6

1 Plunge the tomatoes into boiling water for 30 seconds, then refresh in cold water. Peel away the skins and chop roughly.

2 Heat a little of the oil in a large, heavy-based pan and fry the onions for 5 minutes. Add the peppers and fry for a further 2 minutes. Drain. Add the aubergines and more oil and fry gently for 5 minutes. Add the remaining oil and courgettes and fry for 3 minutes. Drain.

3 Add the garlic and tomatoes to the pan with the bay leaves and thyme and a little salt and pepper. Cook gently until the tomatoes have softened and are turning pulpy.

4 Return all the vegetables to the pan and cook gently, stirring frequently, for about 15 minutes, until fairly pulpy but retaining a little texture. Season with more salt and pepper to taste.

COOK'S TIP
There are no specific quantities for the vegetables when making ratatouille so you can, to a large extent, vary the quantities and types of vegetables depending on what you have in the fridge. If the tomatoes are a little tasteless, add 30–45ml/2–3 tbsp tomato purée and a dash of sugar to the mixture along with the tomatoes.

SPINACH WITH RAISINS AND PINE NUTS

Raisins and pine nuts are frequent partners in Spanish recipes. Here, tossed with wilted spinach and croûtons, they make a delicious snack or main meal accompaniment.

50g/2oz/⅓ cup raisins
1 thick slice crusty white bread
45ml/3 tbsp olive oil
25g/1oz/⅓ cup pine nuts
500g/1¼lb young spinach,
stalks removed
2 garlic cloves, crushed
salt and ground black pepper

SERVES 4

1. Put the raisins in a small bowl with boiling water and leave to soak for 10 minutes. Drain.

2. Cut the bread into cubes and discard the crusts. Heat 30ml/ 2 tbsp of the oil and fry the bread until golden. Drain.

3. Heat the remaining oil in the pan. Fry the pine nuts until beginning to colour. Add the spinach and garlic and cook quickly, turning the spinach until it has just wilted.

4. Toss in the raisins and season lightly with salt and pepper. Transfer to a warmed serving dish. Scatter with croûtons and serve hot.

VARIATION
Use Swiss chard or spinach beet instead of the spinach, cooking them a little longer.

SPICED TURNIPS WITH SPINACH AND TOMATOES

Sweet baby turnips, tender spinach and ripe tomatoes make tempting partners in this simple Eastern Mediterranean vegetable stew.

450g/1lb plum or other
well-flavoured tomatoes
60ml/4 tbsp olive oil
2 onions, sliced
450g/1lb baby turnips, peeled
5ml/1 tsp paprika
2.5ml/½ tsp caster sugar
60ml/4 tbsp chopped fresh coriander
450g/1lb fresh young spinach,
stalks removed
salt and ground black pepper

SERVES 6

1 Plunge the tomatoes into a bowl of boiling water for 30 seconds, then refresh in a bowl of cold water. Peel away the tomato skins and chop roughly. Heat the olive oil in a large frying pan or sauté pan and fry the onion slices for about 5 minutes until golden.

2 Add the baby turnips, tomatoes and paprika to the pan with 60ml/4 tbsp water and cook until the tomatoes are pulpy. Cover with a lid and continue cooking until the baby turnips have softened.

3 Stir in the sugar and coriander, then add the spinach and a little salt and pepper and cook for a further 2–3 minutes until the spinach has wilted. Serve warm or cold.

STUFFED VINE LEAVES WITH GARLIC YOGURT

An old Greek recipe which comes in many guises. This meatless version is highly flavoured with fresh herbs, lemon and a little chilli.

225g/8oz packet preserved vine leaves
1 onion, finely chopped
½ bunch of spring onions, trimmed
and finely chopped
60ml/4 tbsp chopped fresh parsley
10 large mint sprigs, chopped
finely grated rind of 1 lemon
2.5ml/½ tsp crushed dried chillies
7.5ml/1½ tsp fennel seeds, crushed
175g/6oz/scant 1 cup long grain rice
120ml/4fl oz/½ cup olive oil
150ml/¼ pint/⅔ cup thick
natural yogurt
2 garlic cloves, crushed
salt
lemon wedges and mint leaves,
to garnish (optional)

SERVES 6

1 Rinse the vine leaves in plenty of cold water. Put in a bowl, cover with boiling water and leave for 10 minutes. Drain thoroughly.

2 Mix together the onion, spring onions, parsley, mint, lemon, chilli, fennel, rice and 25ml/1½ tbsp of the olive oil. Mix thoroughly and season with salt.

3 Place a vine leaf, veined side facing upwards, on a work surface and cut off any stalk. Place a heaped teaspoonful of the rice mixture near the stalk end of the leaf.

4 Fold the stalk end of the leaf over the rice filling, then fold over the sides and carefully roll up into a neat cigar shape.

5 Repeat with the remaining filling to make about 28 stuffed leaves. If some of the vine leaves are quite small, use two and patch them together to make parcels of the same size.

6 Place any remaining leaves in the base of a large heavy-based saucepan. Pack the stuffed leaves in a single layer in the pan. Spoon over the remaining oil then add about 300ml/½ pint/1¼ cups boiling water.

COOK'S TIP
To check that the rice is cooked, lift out one stuffed leaf and cut in half. The rice should have expanded and softened to make a firm parcel. If necessary, cook the stuffed leaves a little longer, adding boiling water if the pan is becoming dry.

7 Place a small plate over the leaves to keep them submerged in the water. Cover the pan and cook on a very low heat for 45 minutes.

8 Mix together the yogurt and garlic and put in a small serving dish. Transfer the stuffed leaves to a serving plate and garnish with lemon wedges and mint, if you like. Serve with the garlic yogurt.

SPICY CHICK-PEA AND AUBERGINE STEW

This is a Lebanese dish, but similar recipes are found all over the Mediterranean.

3 large aubergines, cubed
200g/7oz/1 cup chick-peas, soaked
overnight
60ml/4 tbsp olive oil
3 garlic cloves, chopped
2 large onions, chopped
2.5ml/½ tsp ground cumin
2.5ml/½ tsp ground cinnamon
2.5ml/½ tsp ground coriander
3 x 400g/14oz cans chopped tomatoes
salt and ground black pepper
cooked rice, to serve

FOR THE GARNISH
30ml/2 tbsp olive oil
1 onion, sliced
1 garlic clove, sliced
sprigs of coriander

SERVES 4

 1 Place the aubergines in a colander and sprinkle them with salt. Sit the colander in a bowl and leave for 30 minutes, to allow the bitter juices to escape. Rinse with cold water and dry on kitchen paper.

2 Drain the chick-peas and put in a pan with enough water to cover. Bring to the boil and simmer for 30 minutes, or until tender. Drain.

3 Heat the oil in a large pan. Add the garlic and onion and cook gently, until soft. Add the spices and cook, stirring, for a few seconds. Add the aubergine and stir to coat with the spices and onion. Cook for 5 minutes. Add the tomatoes and chick-peas and season with salt and pepper. Cover and simmer for 20 minutes.

4 To make the garnish, heat the oil in a frying pan and, when very hot, add the sliced onion and garlic. Fry until golden and crisp. Serve the stew with rice, topped with the onion and garlic and garnished with coriander.

SPANISH POTATOES

This is an adaptation of a peppery potato dish, of which there are several versions. All of them are fried and mildly spiced with the added tang of wine vinegar. Serve with cold meats or as a tapas.

675g/1½ lb small new potatoes
75ml/5 tbsp olive oil
2 garlic cloves, sliced
2.5ml/½ tsp crushed chillies
2.5ml/½ tsp ground cumin
10ml/2 tsp paprika
30ml/2 tbsp red or white
wine vinegar
1 red or green pepper, seeded
and sliced
coarse sea salt, to serve (optional)

SERVES 4

1 Cook the potatoes in boiling salted water until almost tender. Drain and, if preferred, peel them. Cut into chunks.

2 Heat the oil in a large frying or sauté pan and fry the potatoes, turning them frequently until golden.

3 Meanwhile, crush together the garlic, chillies and cumin using a pestle and mortar. Mix with the paprika and wine vinegar.

4 Add the garlic mixture to the potatoes with the sliced pepper and cook, stirring, for 2 minutes. Serve warm, or leave until cold. Scatter with coarse sea salt, if you like, to serve.

SALADS

Summer and salads are synonymous, and
nowhere is there a wider variety of these
flavoursome dishes than in the Mediterranean.

The climate of the Mediterranean countries has ensured that salads and cold dishes have always been popular. There is an abundance of wonderful ingredients, particularly vegetables, which are combined to produce delicious results. In its simplest form, a salad in France, Spain or Italy would consist of lettuce, or perhaps a mixture of a few different salad leaves, dressed with vinaigrette. A salad may be eaten after the main course, often before the cheese is served. Vinaigrette is the basic salad dressing. Originally a French classic, it is now used world-wide. As its name suggests, vinegar is a main ingredient, combined with three times its quantity of olive

RIGHT: Visiting a Turkish market is more than a mere shopping trip; it's a chance to catch up on local news.

LEFT: Some of these plump Moroccan olives will find their way into salads, but the majority will be pressed for oil.

oil, and seasoned with salt and pepper. There are many variations, using different ingredients such as lemon juice, mustard, herbs, garlic and cream, and the types of oils and vinegars can be varied too. Extra virgin olive oil gives the finest flavour of all the olive oils, but a mixture of peanut oil and olive oil will produce a lighter dressing. Nut oils, such as walnut, complement salads containing nuts. The Italians favour a good red wine vinegar, but there is also the sour/sweet flavour of balsamic vinegar to consider – delicious with grilled vegetables. Spanish sherry vinegar is another good flavour to try. Herb-infused vinegars are also useful, particularly if the fresh herbs are unavailable.

There is an abundant variety of salad leaves in the Mediterranean, ranging in colour, taste and texture. The French favour a mixture of leaves called "mesclun", which can be bought in the markets by the handful. Dandelion leaves are popular too, as well as frisée, chicory, oak leaf lettuce and many more. In Italy, radicchio and rocket are preferred, and Spaniards favour romaine lettuce. In the

ABOVE: A quiet landscape near Carmona, in the beautiful region of Andalusia.

Middle East, however, leaf salads are less popular. Salads of cooked or raw vegetables, dressed with a lemony vinaigrette, are more typical of these countries. Fresh herbs also play an important part, sometimes served alone, between courses, to cleanse the palate. These basic leaf salads are spontaneous, depending on what is available in the market, and need no recipes.

The markets of the Mediterranean offer some of the best vegetables and fruit in the world. From huge vine-ripened tomatoes to tiny artichokes, all are lovingly displayed, waiting to be picked up and dropped into a basket to be taken home. The inspiration for salads is endless. Fruit too, is included; grapes and oranges make refreshing additions to some of our recipes.

Apart from the simple salads, there are the composed salads – specific ingredients, with a special dressing, which are dishes on their own, to be eaten as a lunch dish, or perhaps a starter. These salads include all sorts of foodstuffs: olives, sausage, nuts, cheese, anchovies; morsels chosen for a contrast in taste, texture and colour.

This chapter includes some of the classic salads of the region, including Salad Niçoise, and Greek Salad, which are sure to transport anyone who has eaten them in their native countries straight to a little village on the coast of the Mediterranean. Some salads are substantial enough to be served as a main meal, such as Roasted Peppers with Tomatoes and Anchovies or Broad Bean, Mushroom and Chorizo salad. Bread and a glass of wine should complete the picture!

ROASTED PEPPERS WITH TOMATOES AND ANCHOVIES

This is a Sicilian-style salad, using some typical ingredients from the Italian island. The flavour improves if the salad is made and dressed an hour or two before serving.

1 red pepper
1 yellow pepper
4 sun-dried tomatoes in oil, drained
4 ripe plum tomatoes, sliced
2 canned anchovies, drained
and chopped
15ml/1 tbsp capers, drained
15ml/1 tbsp pine nuts
1 garlic clove, very thinly sliced

FOR THE DRESSING
75ml/5 tbsp extra virgin olive oil
15ml/1 tbsp balsamic vinegar
5ml/1 tsp lemon juice
chopped fresh mixed herbs
salt and ground black pepper

SERVES 4

1 Cut the peppers in half, and remove the seeds and stalks. Cut into quarters and cook, skin side up, under a hot grill until the skin chars. Transfer to a bowl, and cover with a plate. Leave to cool. Peel the peppers and cut into strips.

2 Thinly slice the sun-dried tomatoes. Arrange the peppers and fresh tomatoes on a serving dish. Scatter over the anchovies, sun-dried tomatoes, capers, pine nuts and garlic.

3 To make the dressing, mix together the olive oil, vinegar, lemon juice and chopped herbs and season with salt and pepper. Pour over the salad just before serving.

SWEET AND SOUR ONION SALAD

This recipe is primarily from Provence in the south of France but there are influences from other Mediterranean countries, too.

450g/1lb baby onions, peeled
50ml/2fl oz/¼ cup wine vinegar
45ml/3 tbsp olive oil
40g/1½oz/3 tbsp caster sugar
45ml/3 tbsp tomato purée
1 bay leaf
2 parsley sprigs
65g/2½oz/½ cup raisins
salt and ground black pepper

SERVES 6

1 Put all the ingredients in a pan with 300ml/½ pint/1¼ cups water. Bring to the boil and simmer gently, uncovered, for 45 minutes, or until the onions are tender and most of the liquid has evaporated.

2 Remove the bay leaf and parsley, check the seasoning, and transfer to a serving dish. Serve at room temperature.

GREEK SALAD

ne who has spent a holiday in Greece will have eaten a version of this salad – the Greeks'
nt to a mixed salad. Its success relies on using the freshest of ingredients, and a good olive oil.

1 small cos lettuce, sliced
450g/1lb well-flavoured tomatoes, cut
into eighths
1 cucumber, seeded and chopped
200g/7oz feta cheese, crumbled
4 spring onions, sliced
50g/2oz/½ cup black olives, stoned
and halved

FOR THE DRESSING
90ml/6 tbsp good olive oil
25ml/1½ tbsp lemon juice
salt and ground black pepper

SERVES 6

1 Put all the main salad ingredients into a large bowl. Whisk together the olive oil and lemon juice, then season with salt and pepper, and pour the dressing over the salad. Mix well and serve immediately.

SPICED AUBERGINE SALAD

Serve this Middle-Eastern influenced salad with warm pitta bread as a starter or to accompany a main
course rice pilaff.

2 small aubergines, sliced
75ml/5 tbsp olive oil
50ml/2fl oz/¼ cup red wine vinegar
2 garlic cloves, crushed
15ml/1 tbsp lemon juice
2.5ml/½ tsp ground cumin
2.5ml/½ tsp ground coriander
½ cucumber, thinly sliced
2 well-flavoured tomatoes,
thinly sliced
30ml/2 tbsp natural yogurt
salt and ground black pepper
chopped flat leaf parsley, to garnish

SERVES 4

2 Mix together the remaining oil, vinegar, garlic, lemon juice, cumin and coriander. Season with salt and pepper and mix thoroughly. Add the warm aubergines, stir well and chill for at least 2 hours. Add the cucumber and tomatoes. Transfer to a serving dish and spoon the yogurt on top. Sprinkle with parsley.

1 Preheat the grill. Brush the aubergine slices lightly with some of the oil and cook under a high heat, turning once, until golden and tender. Cut into quarters.

MOROCCAN DATE, ORANGE AND CARROT SALAD

A colourful and unusual salad with exotic ingredients – fresh dates and orange flower water – combined with crisp leaves, carrots, oranges and toasted almonds.

1 Little Gem lettuce
2 carrots, finely grated
2 oranges
115g/4oz fresh dates, stoned and cut
into eighths, lengthways
25g/1oz/¼ cup toasted whole
almonds, chopped
30ml/2 tbsp lemon juice
5ml/1 tsp caster sugar
1.5ml/¼ tsp salt
15ml/1 tbsp orange flower water

SERVES 4

☐1 Separate the lettuce leaves and arrange them in the bottom of a salad bowl or on individual serving plates. Place the grated carrot in a mound on top.

☐2 Peel and segment the oranges and arrange them around the carrot. Pile the dates on top, then sprinkle with the almonds. Mix together the lemon juice, sugar, salt and orange flower water and sprinkle over the salad. Serve chilled.

MOROCCAN COOKED SALAD

A version of a North African favourite, this cooked salad is served as a side dish with a main course.
Make this one the day before to improve the flavour.

2 well-flavoured tomatoes, quartered
2 onions, chopped
½ cucumber, halved lengthways,
seeded and sliced
1 green pepper, halved, seeded
and chopped
30ml/2 tbsp lemon juice
45ml/3 tbsp olive oil
2 garlic cloves, crushed
30ml/2 tbsp chopped fresh coriander
salt and ground black pepper
sprigs of coriander, to garnish

SERVES 4

1 Put the tomatoes, onions, cucumber and green pepper into a pan, add 60ml/4 tbsp water and simmer for 5 minutes. Leave to cool.

2 Mix together the lemon juice, olive oil and garlic. Strain the vegetables, then transfer to a bowl. Pour over the dressing, season with salt and pepper and stir in the chopped coriander. Serve at once, garnished with coriander, if you like.

PANZANELLA

In this lively Italian speciality, a sweet tangy blend of tomato juice, rich olive oil and red wine vinegar is soaked up in a colourful salad of roasted peppers, anchovies and toasted ciabatta.

225g/8oz ciabatta (about ⅔ loaf)
150ml/¼ pint/⅔ cup olive oil
3 red peppers
3 yellow peppers
675g/1½lb ripe plum tomatoes
4 garlic cloves, crushed
60ml/4 tbsp red wine vinegar
50g/2oz can anchovy fillets
50g/2oz capers
115g/4oz/1 cup pitted black olives
salt and ground black pepper
basil leaves, to garnish

SERVES 4–6

1 Preheat the oven to 200°C/ 400°F/Gas 6. Cut the ciabatta into 2cm/¾in chunks and drizzle with 50ml/2fl oz/¼ cup of the oil. Grill lightly until just golden.

2 Put the peppers on a foil-lined baking sheet and bake for about 45 minutes until the skin begins to char. Remove from the oven, cover with a cloth and leave to cool slightly.

3 Pull the skin off the peppers and cut them into quarters, discarding the stalk ends and seeds. Drain and then roughly chop the anchovies. Set aside.

4 To make the tomato dressing, peel and halve the tomatoes. Scoop the seeds into a sieve set over a bowl. Using the back of a spoon, press the tomato pulp in the sieve to extract as much juice as possible. Discard the pulp and add the remaining oil, the garlic and vinegar to the juices.

5 Layer the toasted bread, peppers, tomatoes, anchovies, capers and olives in a large salad bowl. Season the tomato dressing with salt and pepper and pour it over the salad. Leave to stand for about 30 minutes. Serve garnished with plenty of basil leaves.

RADICCHIO, ARTICHOKE AND WALNUT SALAD

The distinctive, earthy taste of Jerusalem artichokes makes a lovely contrast to the sharp freshness of radicchio and lemon. Serve warm or cold as an accompaniment to grilled steak or barbecued meats.

1 large radicchio or 150g/5oz radicchio leaves
40g/1½oz/6 tbsp walnut pieces
45ml/3 tbsp walnut oil
500g/1¼lb Jerusalem artichokes
pared rind and juice of 1 lemon
coarse sea salt and ground black pepper
flat leaf parsley, to garnish (optional)

SERVES 4

1 If using a whole radicchio, cut it into 8–10 wedges. Put the wedges or leaves in a flameproof dish. Scatter over the walnuts, then spoon over the oil and season. Grill for 2–3 minutes.

2 Peel the artichokes and cut up any large ones so the pieces are all roughly the same size. Add the artichokes to a pan of boiling salted water with half the lemon juice and cook for 5–7 minutes until tender. Drain. Preheat the grill to high.

3 Toss the artichokes into the salad with the remaining lemon juice and the pared rind. Season with coarse salt and pepper. Grill until beginning to brown. Serve at once garnished with torn pieces of parsley, if you like.

CACIK

This refreshing yogurt dish is served all over the Eastern Mediterranean, whether as part of a mezze with marinated olives and pitta bread, or as an accompaniment to meat dishes. Greek tzatziki is very similar.

1 small cucumber
300ml/½ pint/1¼ cups thick
natural yogurt
3 garlic cloves, crushed
30ml/2 tbsp chopped fresh mint
30ml/2 tbsp chopped fresh dill
or parsley
salt and ground black pepper
mint or parsley and dill, to garnish
olive oil, olives and pitta bread,
to serve

SERVES 6

1 Finely chop the cucumber and layer in a colander with plenty of salt. Leave for 30 minutes. Wash the cucumber in several changes of cold water and drain thoroughly. Pat dry on kitchen paper.

2 Mix together the yogurt, garlic and herbs and season with salt and pepper. Stir in the cucumber. Garnish with herbs, drizzle over a little olive oil and serve with olives and pitta bread.

BROWN BEAN SALAD

Brown beans, sometimes called "ful medames", are widely used in Egyptian cookery, and are occasionally seen in health food shops here. Dried broad beans, black or red kidney beans make a good substitute.

350g/12oz/1½ cups dried brown beans
3 thyme sprigs
2 bay leaves
1 onion, halved
4 garlic cloves, crushed
7.5ml/1½ tsp cumin seeds, crushed
3 spring onions, finely chopped
90ml/6 tbsp chopped fresh parsley
20ml/4 tsp lemon juice
90ml/6 tbsp olive oil
3 hard-boiled eggs, shelled and roughly chopped
1 pickled cucumber, roughly chopped
salt and ground black pepper

SERVES 6

1   Put the beans in a bowl with plenty of cold water and leave to soak overnight. Drain, transfer to a saucepan and cover with fresh water. Bring to the boil and boil rapidly for 10 minutes.

2   Reduce the heat and add the thyme, bay leaves and onion. Simmer very gently for about 1 hour until tender. Drain and discard the herbs and onion.

COOK'S TIP
The cooking time for dried beans can vary considerably. They may need only 45 minutes, or a lot longer.

3   Mix together the garlic, cumin, spring onions, parsley, lemon juice, oil and add a little salt and pepper. Pour over the beans and toss the ingredients lightly together.

4   Gently stir in the eggs and cucumber and serve at once.

WARM BROAD BEAN AND FETA SALAD

This recipe is loosely based on a typical medley of fresh-tasting Greek salad ingredients — broad beans, tomatoes and feta cheese. It's lovely warm or cold as a starter or main course accompaniment.

900g/2lb broad beans, shelled, or
350g/12oz shelled frozen beans
60ml/4 tbsp olive oil
175g/6oz plum tomatoes, halved, or
quartered if large
4 garlic cloves, crushed
115g/4oz firm feta cheese, cut
into chunks
45ml/3 tbsp chopped fresh dill
12 black olives
salt and ground black pepper
chopped fresh dill, to garnish

SERVES 4–6

1 Cook the fresh or frozen broad beans in boiling, salted water until just tender. Drain and set aside.

2 Meanwhile, heat the oil in a heavy-based frying pan and add the tomatoes and garlic. Cook until the tomatoes are beginning to colour.

3 Add the feta to the pan and toss the ingredients together for 1 minute. Mix with the drained beans, dill, olives and salt and pepper. Serve garnished with chopped dill.

HALLOUMI AND GRAPE SALAD

In Eastern Europe, firm salty halloumi cheese is often served fried for breakfast or supper. In this recipe it's tossed with sweet, juicy grapes which really complement its distinctive flavour.

FOR THE DRESSING
60ml/4 tbsp olive oil
15ml/1 tbsp lemon juice
2.5ml/½ tsp caster sugar
salt and ground black pepper
15ml/1 tbsp chopped fresh thyme or dill

FOR THE SALAD
150g/5oz mixed green salad leaves
75g/3oz seedless green grapes
75g/3oz seedless black grapes
250g/9oz halloumi cheese
45ml/3 tbsp olive oil
fresh young thyme leaves or dill,
to garnish

SERVES 4

1 To make the dressing, mix together the olive oil, lemon juice and sugar. Season. Stir in the thyme or dill and set aside.

2 Toss together the salad leaves and the green and black grapes, then transfer to a large serving plate.

3 Thinly slice the cheese. Heat the oil in a large frying pan. Add the cheese and fry briefly until turning golden on the underside. Turn the cheese with a fish slice and cook the other side.

4 Arrange the cheese over the salad. Pour over the dressing and garnish with thyme or dill.

SALAD NICOISE

Made with good quality ingredients, this Provençal salad makes a simple yet unbeatable summer lunch or supper dish. Serve with country-style bread and chilled white wine.

FOR THE DRESSING
90ml/6 tbsp extra virgin olive oil
2 garlic cloves, crushed
15ml/1 tbsp white wine vinegar
salt and ground black pepper

FOR THE SALAD
115g/4oz French beans, trimmed
115g/4oz mixed salad leaves
½ small cucumber, thinly sliced
4 ripe tomatoes, quartered
200g/7oz can tuna in oil, drained
50g/2oz can anchovies, drained
4 eggs, hard-boiled
½ bunch radishes, trimmed
50g/2oz/½ cup small black olives
flat leaf parsley, to garnish

SERVES 4

1 To make the dressing, whisk together the oil, garlic and vinegar and season to taste with salt and pepper.

2 Halve the French beans and cook in a saucepan of boiling water for 2 minutes until only just tender, then drain.

3 Mix the salad leaves, cucumber, tomatoes and beans in a large, shallow salad bowl. Flake the tuna. Halve the anchovies lengthways. Shell and quarter the eggs.

4 Scatter the radishes, tuna, anchovies, eggs and olives over the salad. Pour over the dressing and toss together lightly. Serve garnished with parsley.

SPANISH ASPARAGUS AND ORANGE SALAD

Complicated salad dressings are rarely found in Spain — they simply rely on the wonderful flavour of a good quality olive oil.

225g/8oz asparagus, trimmed and cut
into 5cm/2in pieces
2 large oranges
2 well-flavoured tomatoes, cut
into eighths
50g/2oz romaine lettuce leaves,
shredded
30ml/2 tbsp extra virgin olive oil
2.5ml/½ tsp sherry vinegar
salt and ground black pepper

SERVES 4

COOK'S TIP
Cos or Little Gem lettuce can be used
in place of romaine.

1 Cook the asparagus in boiling, salted water for 3–4 minutes, until just tender. Drain and refresh under cold water.

2 Grate the rind from half an orange and reserve. Peel all the oranges and cut into segments. Squeeze out the juice from the membrane and reserve the juice.

3 Put the asparagus, orange segments, tomatoes and lettuce into a salad bowl. Mix together the oil and vinegar and add 15ml/1 tbsp of the reserved orange juice and 5ml/1 tsp of the rind *(left)*. Season with salt and pepper. Just before serving, pour the dressing over the salad and mix gently to coat.

GLOBE ARTICHOKES WITH GREEN BEANS AND AIOLI

Just like the French aïoli, there are many recipes for the Spanish equivalent. This one is exceptionally garlicky, a perfect partner to freshly cooked vegetables.

FOR THE AIOLI
*6 large garlic cloves, sliced
10ml/2 tsp white wine vinegar
250ml/8fl oz/1 cup olive oil
salt and ground black pepper*

FOR THE SALAD
*225g/8oz green beans
3 small globe artichokes
15ml/1 tbsp olive oil
pared rind of 1 lemon
coarse salt for sprinkling
lemon wedges, to garnish*

SERVES 4–6

1 To make the aïoli, put the garlic and vinegar in a blender or mini food processor. With the machine switched on, gradually pour in the olive oil until the mixture is thickened and smooth. (Alternatively, crush the garlic to a paste with the vinegar and gradually beat in the oil using a hand whisk.) Season with salt and pepper to taste.

2 To make the salad, cook the beans in boiling water for 1–2 minutes until slightly softened. Drain.

3 Trim the artichoke stalks close to the base. Cook the artichokes in a large pan of salted water for about 30 minutes, or until you can easily pull away a leaf from the base. Drain well.

4 Using a sharp knife, halve the artichokes lengthways and ease out the choke using a teaspoon.

5 Arrange the artichokes and beans on serving plates and drizzle with the oil. Scatter with the lemon rind and season with coarse salt and a little pepper. Spoon the aïoli into the artichoke hearts and serve warm, garnished with lemon wedges. To eat artichokes, pull the leaves from the base one at a time and use to scoop a little of the sauce. It is only the fleshy end of each leaf that is eaten as well as the base or "heart" of the artichoke.

COOK'S TIP
Mediterranean baby artichokes are sometimes available and are perfect for this kind of salad as, unlike the larger ones, they can be eaten whole. Cook them until just tender, then cut in half to serve.
Canned artichoke hearts, thoroughly drained and sliced, can be substituted when fresh ones are not available.

BROAD BEAN, MUSHROOM AND CHORIZO SALAD

Broad beans are used in both their fresh and dried forms in various Mediterranean countries. This Spanish salad could be served as either a first course or lunch dish.

225g/8oz shelled broad beans
175g/6oz chorizo sausage
60ml/4 tbsp extra virgin olive oil
225g/8oz brown cap
mushrooms, sliced
handful of fresh chives
salt and ground black pepper

SERVES 4

1 Cook the broad beans in boiling, salted water for about 7–8 minutes. Drain and refresh under cold water.

2 Remove the skin from the sausage and cut it into small chunks. Heat the oil in a frying pan, add the chorizo and cook for 2–3 minutes. Tip the chorizo and oil into the mushrooms and mix well. Leave to cool. Chop half the chives. If the beans are large, peel away the tough outer skins. Stir the beans and snipped chives into the mushroom mixture, and season to taste. Serve at room temperature, garnished with the remaining chives.

AVOCADO, ORANGE AND ALMOND SALAD

The Mediterranean is not particularly known for its avocados, but the climate is perfect and they are grown in many parts of the region. This salad has a Spanish influence.

2 oranges
2 well-flavoured tomatoes
2 small avocados
60ml/4 tbsp extra virgin olive oil
30ml/2 tbsp lemon juice
15ml/1 tbsp chopped fresh parsley
1 small onion, sliced into rings
salt and ground black pepper
25g/1oz/¼ cup flaked almonds
and 10–12 black olives,
to garnish

SERVES 4

1 Peel the oranges and slice into thick rounds. Plunge the tomatoes into boiling water for 30 seconds, then refresh in cold water. Peel away the skins, cut into quarters, remove the seeds and chop roughly.

2 Cut the avocados in half, remove the stones and carefully peel away the skin. Cut into chunks.

3 Mix together the olive oil, lemon juice and parsley. Season with salt and pepper. Toss the avocados and tomatoes in half of the dressing.

4 Arrange the sliced oranges on a plate and scatter over the onion rings. Drizzle with the rest of the dressing. Spoon the avocados, tomatoes, almonds and olives on top.

FISH AND
SEAFOOD

*Mediterranean fishermen reap a rich harvest of
fish and seafood, which are often simply grilled or
fried, or used as the basis of a soup or stew.*

The Mediterranean sea is tiny in relation to the world's larger seas and oceans. It is also relatively shallow, warm, low in natural food supplies and more polluted. Despite all these factors, the Mediterranean has hundreds of different species of fish and crustacea, marketed in the Mediterranean and beyond. Visit a large fish market in any part of the region and you will be amazed at the fantastic variety of fish, many of which are completely unknown, except to the locals and, of course, the fishermen themselves.

ABOVE: Fishermen in Crete bring home the day's catch, packed in salt.

LEFT: Safely back in harbour, a Cretan fishing boat bobs gently on the calm sea.

A visit to a Mediterranean restaurant, bar or taverna, illustrates how this freshly caught fish, cooked simply, can be quite unbeatable. Few of us ever forget the arrival of a hot, steaming bowl of garlicky mussels or crisp prawns, dripping in garlic and olive oil. Perfectly fresh fish, grilled or barbecued with a basting of olive oil, garlic and herbs, needs little more embellishment, except perhaps a crisp salad and light wine.

On a more elaborate scale, fish stew and soups are typically Mediterranean. A varied mixture of fish such as conger eel, gurnard, John Dory, monkfish, bass, bream and red mullet is combined with aromatic flavourings like saffron, herbs, garlic and orange peel and cooked in an intensely flavoured fish stock made from all fish trimmings. The *bourride* of France and the *brodetto* of Italy are classic examples but similar variations can be found all over the Mediterranean.

Small oily fish thrive in the Mediterranean and the

ABOVE: A Moroccan cook patiently prepares the family meal of fish kebabs.

delicious as a light snack or starter with a scattering of *gremolata* (a blend of garlic, parsley and lemon zest) or simply squeezed with lemon. The Spanish also love fried fish and use much the same technique, sometimes simply dredging the fish with seasoned flour before frying in light olive oil.

Taking into consideration the availability of so much fresh produce it is surprising that salt cod is so well loved in various parts of the Mediterranean; the kite-shaped, leathery pieces are a common sight in many marketplaces. The Spanish and Portuguese fished for cod in the Atlantic, salted it and sun-dried it at sea as a means of preservation. These familiar, stiff yellow-tinged boards of fish, which once were associated with the frugal eating of Lent, are now a highly esteemed luxury. Perhaps the most famous dish is the *brandade* of France, a smooth purée of salt cod, flavoured with garlic and olive oil.

On the eastern side of the Mediterranean the types of fish available are much the same, although the cooking methods vary. Baking fish whole is the most widespread practice, often on a bed of tomatoes, lemons, onions, herbs, and sometimes with slightly sweet and spicy flavourings such as raisins and cinnamon. *Plaki* is a well-loved example, perfect for fish such as grey mullet, sea bream and bass, which absorbs all the wonderful flavours of the accompanying ingredients. Middle Eastern and North African fish dishes emphasize the accompanying sauce – the choice of fish being the pick of the catch. A simple blend of tahini with olive oil and lemon juice is very classical.

Squid and octopus both play an important role in Mediterranean cookery. Squid, from the tiniest, which are lovely seared in olive oil with garlic and herbs, to huge specimens, rich with stuffings, typify Mediterranean cooking techniques. Octopus too, is highly esteemed particularly in the eastern Mediterranean where it is frequently stewed with red wine or used in salads.

freshly grilled or barbecued sardines prepared in cafes and tavernas around the region cannot be rivalled anywhere else in the world. Sardines and large anchovies are sometimes stuffed with a slightly tangy mixture of ingredients, such as capers, olives, pine nuts, lemons and dried fruit, that provides a perfect contrast to the rich oiliness of the fish itself. Other interesting recipes are the short term preserving of fried sardines in olive oil and vinegar or the delicious combination of sardines with fresh herbs and spaghetti or macaroni.

The technique of frying fish in a light batter is typical of the Mediterranean. Fritto Misto is an Italian version in which a medley of seafood, such as mussels, squid, red mullet, prawns and whitebait, is coated in a light crisp batter and deep fried. When served piping hot, this is

PAN-FRIED RED MULLET WITH BASIL AND CITRUS

Red mullet is popular all over the Mediterranean. This Italian recipe combines it with oranges and lemons, which grow in abundance.

4 red mullet, about 225g/8oz each, filleted
90ml/6 tbsp olive oil
10 peppercorns, crushed
2 oranges, one peeled and sliced and one squeezed
1 lemon
30ml/2 tbsp plain flour
15g/½oz/1 tbsp butter
2 drained canned anchovies, chopped
60ml/4 tbsp shredded fresh basil
salt and ground black pepper

SERVES 4

1 Place the fish fillets in a shallow dish in a single layer. Pour over the olive oil and sprinkle with the crushed peppercorns. Lay the orange slices on top of the fish. Cover the dish, and leave to marinate in the fridge for at least 4 hours.

2 Halve the lemon. Remove the skin and pith from one half using a small sharp knife, and slice thinly. Squeeze the juice from the other half.

COOK'S TIP
If you prefer, use other fish fillets for this dish, such as lemon sole, haddock or hake.

3 Lift the fish out of the marinade, and pat dry on kitchen paper. Reserve the marinade and orange slices. Season the fish with salt and pepper and dust lightly with flour.

4 Heat 45ml/3 tbsp of the marinade in a frying pan. Add the fish and fry for 2 minutes on each side. Remove from the pan and keep warm. Discard the marinade that is left in the pan.

5 Melt the butter in the pan with any of the remaining original marinade. Add the anchovies and cook until completely softened.

6 Stir in the orange and lemon juice, then check the seasoning and simmer until slightly reduced. Stir in the basil. Pour the sauce over the fish and garnish with the reserved orange slices and the lemon slices.

SEAFOOD RISOTTO

Risotto is one of Italy's most popular rice dishes and it is made with everything from pumpkin to squid ink. On the Mediterranean shores, seafood is the most obvious addition.

60ml/4 tbsp sunflower oil
1 onion, chopped
2 garlic cloves, crushed
225g/8oz/generous 1 cup arborio rice
105ml/7 tbsp white wine
1.5 litres/2½ pints/6¼ cups hot fish stock
350g/12oz mixed seafood, such as raw prawns, mussels, squid rings or clams
grated rind of ½ lemon
30ml/2 tbsp tomato purée
15ml/1 tbsp chopped fresh parsley
salt and ground black pepper

SERVES 4

1 Heat the oil in a heavy-based pan, add the onion and garlic and cook until soft. Add the rice and stir to coat the grains with oil. Add the wine and cook over a moderate heat, stirring, for a few minutes until absorbed.

2 Add 150ml/¼ pint/⅔ cup of the hot stock and cook, stirring constantly, until the liquid is absorbed by the rice. Continue stirring and adding stock in 150ml/¼ pint/⅔ cup quantities, until half is left. This should take about 10 minutes.

3 Stir in the seafood and cook for 2–3 minutes. Add the remaining stock as before, until the rice is cooked. It should be quite creamy and the grains *al dente*.

4 Stir in the lemon rind, tomato purée and parsley. Season with salt and pepper and serve warm.

ITALIAN PRAWN SKEWERS

Simple and delicious mouthfuls from the Amalfi Coast.

900g/2lb raw tiger prawns, peeled
60ml/4 tbsp olive oil
45ml/3 tbsp vegetable oil
75g/3oz/1¼ cups very fine dry breadcrumbs
1 garlic clove, crushed
15ml/1 tbsp chopped fresh parsley
salt and ground black pepper
lemon wedges, to serve

SERVES 4

1 Slit the prawns down their backs and remove the dark vein. Rinse in cold water and pat dry.

2 Put the olive oil and vegetable oil in a large bowl and add the prawns, mixing them to coat evenly. Add the breadcrumbs, garlic and parsley and season with salt and pepper. Toss the prawns thoroughly, to give them an even coating of breadcrumbs. Cover and leave to marinate for 1 hour.

3 Thread the prawns on to four metal or wooden skewers, curling them up as you do so, so that the tail is skewered in the middle.

4 Preheat the grill. Place the skewers in the grill pan and cook for about 2 minutes on each side, until the breadcrumbs are golden. Serve with lemon wedges.

BLACK PASTA WITH SQUID SAUCE

Tagliatelle flavoured with squid ink looks amazing and tastes deliciously of the sea. You'll find it in good Italian delicatessens.

105ml/7 tbsp olive oil
2 shallots, chopped
3 garlic cloves, crushed
45ml/3 tbsp chopped fresh parsley
675g/1½lb cleaned squid, cut
into rings and rinsed
150ml/¼ pint/⅔ cup dry white wine
400g/14oz can chopped tomatoes
2.5ml/½ tsp dried chilli flakes
or powder
450g/1lb squid ink tagliatelle
salt and ground black pepper

SERVES 4

1 Heat the oil in a pan and add the shallots. Cook until pale golden, then add the garlic. When the garlic colours a little, add 30ml/2 tbsp of the parsley, stir, then add the squid and stir again. Cook for 3–4 minutes, then add the wine.

2 Simmer for a few seconds, then add the tomatoes and chilli flakes (*right*) and season with salt and pepper. Cover and simmer gently for about 1 hour, until the squid is tender. Add more water if necessary.

3 Cook the pasta in plenty of boiling, salted water, according to the instructions on the packet, or until *al dente*. Drain and return the tagliatelle to the pan. Add the squid sauce and mix well. Sprinkle each serving with the remaining chopped parsley and serve at once.

SICILIAN SPAGHETTI WITH SARDINES

A traditional dish from Sicily, with ingredients that are common to many parts of the Mediterranean.

12 fresh sardines, cleaned and boned
250ml/8fl oz/1 cup olive oil
1 onion, chopped
25g/1oz/¼ cup dill sprigs
50g/2oz/½ cup pine nuts
25g/1oz/2 tbsp raisins, soaked in water
50g/2oz/½ cup fresh breadcrumbs
450g/1lb spaghetti
flour for dusting
salt

SERVES 4

 Wash the sardines and pat dry on kitchen paper. Open them out flat, then cut in half lengthways.

2 Heat 30ml/2 tbsp of the oil in a pan, add the onion and fry until golden. Add the dill and cook gently for a minute or two. Add the pine nuts and raisins and season with salt. Dry-fry the breadcrumbs in a frying pan until golden. Set aside.

3 Cook the spaghetti in boiling, salted water according to the instructions on the packet, until *al dente*. Heat the remaining oil in a pan. Dust the sardines with flour and fry in the hot oil for 2–3 minutes. Drain on kitchen paper.

4 Drain the spaghetti and return to the pan. Add the onion mixture and toss well. Transfer the spaghetti mixture to a serving platter and arrange the fried sardines on top. Sprinkle with the toasted breadcrumbs and serve immediately.

GRILLED KING PRAWNS WITH ROMESCO SAUCE

This sauce, from the Catalan region of Spain, is served with fish and seafood. Its main ingredients are sweet pepper, tomatoes, garlic and almonds.

24 raw king prawns
30–45ml/2–3 tbsp olive oil
flat leaf parsley, to garnish
lemon wedges, to serve

FOR THE SAUCE
2 well-flavoured tomatoes
60ml/4 tbsp olive oil
1 onion, chopped
4 garlic cloves, chopped
1 canned pimiento, chopped
2.5ml/½ tsp dried chilli flakes
or powder
75ml/5 tbsp fish stock
30ml/2 tbsp white wine
10 blanched almonds
15ml/1 tbsp red wine vinegar
salt

SERVES 4

1 To make the sauce, immerse the tomatoes in boiling water for about 30 seconds, then refresh them under cold water. Peel away the skins and roughly chop the flesh.

2 Heat 30ml/2 tbsp of the oil in a pan, add the onion and 3 of the garlic cloves and cook until soft. Add the pimiento, tomatoes, chilli, fish stock and wine, then cover and simmer for 30 minutes.

3 Toast the almonds under the grill until golden. Transfer to a blender or food processor and grind coarsely. Add the remaining 30ml/ 2 tbsp of oil, the vinegar and the last garlic clove and process until evenly combined. Add the tomato and pimiento sauce and process until smooth. Season with salt.

4 Remove the heads from the prawns leaving them otherwise unshelled and, with a sharp knife, slit each one down the back and remove the dark vein. Rinse and pat dry on kitchen paper. Preheat the grill. Toss the prawns in olive oil, then spread out in the grill pan. Grill for about 2–3 minutes on each side, until pink. Arrange on a serving platter with the lemon wedges, and the sauce in a small bowl. Serve at once, garnished with parsley.

GRILLED SEA BASS WITH FENNEL

This dish is served in almost every fish restaurant on the French Mediterranean coast. Traditionally fennel twigs are used but, as they are hard to find, this recipe uses fennel seeds.

❧ ❧

*1 sea bass, weighing 1.75kg/4–4½lb,
cleaned
60–90ml/4–6 tbsp olive oil
10–15ml/2–3 tsp fennel seeds
2 large fennel bulbs, trimmed and
thinly sliced (reserve any fronds)
60ml/4 tbsp Pernod
salt and ground black pepper*

SERVES 6–8

1   With a sharp knife, make three or four deep cuts in both sides of the fish. Brush the fish with olive oil and season with salt and pepper. Sprinkle the fennel seeds in the stomach cavity and in the cuts. Set aside while you cook the fennel.

2   Preheat the grill. Put the slices of fennel in a flameproof dish or on the grill rack and brush with oil. Grill for 4 minutes on each side until tender. Transfer to a large platter.

3   Place the fish on the oiled grill rack and position about 10–13cm/4–5in away from the heat. Grill for 10–12 minutes on each side, brushing with oil occasionally.

4   Transfer the fish to the platter on top of the fennel. Garnish with fennel fronds. Heat the Pernod in a small pan, light it and pour it, flaming, over the fish. Serve at once.

BRANDADE DE MORUE

―

Salt cod is popular in Spain and France and it can be found cooked in a number of ways. This recipe is a purée, flavoured with garlic and olive oil, which is made all over southern France.

675g/1½lb salt cod
300ml/½ pint/1¼ cups olive oil
250ml/8fl oz/1 cup milk
1 garlic clove, crushed
grated nutmeg
lemon juice, to taste
white pepper

FOR THE CROUTES
50ml/2fl oz/¼ cup olive oil
6 slices white bread, crusts removed
1 garlic clove, halved
parsley sprigs, to garnish

SERVES 6

1 Soak the salt cod in cold water for at least 24 hours, changing the water several times. Drain.

2 To make the croûtes, heat the oil in a frying pan. Cut the bread slices in half diagonally and fry in the oil until golden. Drain on kitchen paper, then rub on both sides with garlic.

3 Put the cod in a large pan, with enough cold water to cover. Cover and bring to the boil. Simmer gently for 8–10 minutes, until just tender. Drain and cool. Flake the fish and discard any skin and bone.

4 Heat the oil in a pan until very hot. In a separate pan, scald the milk. Transfer the fish to a blender or food processor and, with the motor running, slowly pour in the hot oil, followed by the milk, until the mixture is smooth and stiff. Transfer to a bowl and beat in the crushed garlic. Season with nutmeg, lemon juice and white pepper. Leave the *brandade* to cool and then chill until almost ready to serve.

5 Spoon the *brandade* into a shallow serving bowl and surround with the croûtes. Garnish with parsley and serve cold.

MOUCLADE OF MUSSELS

This recipe is quite similar to Moules Marinière but has the additional flavouring of fennel and mild curry. Traditionally the mussels are shelled and piled into scallop shells, but nothing beats a bowlful of steaming hot, garlicky mussels, served in their own glistening shells.

1.75kg/4½lb fresh mussels
250ml/8fl oz/1 cup dry white wine
good pinch of grated nutmeg
3 thyme sprigs
2 bay leaves
1 small onion, finely chopped
50g/2oz/¼ cup butter
1 fennel bulb, thinly sliced
4 garlic cloves, crushed
2.5ml/½ tsp curry paste or powder
30ml/2 tbsp plain flour
150ml/¼ pint/⅔ cup double cream
ground black pepper
chopped fresh dill, to garnish

SERVES 6

1 Scrub the mussels, discarding any that are damaged or open ones that do not close when tapped with a knife.

2 Put the wine, nutmeg, thyme, bay leaves and onion in a large saucepan and bring just to the boil. Tip in the mussels and cover with a lid. Cook for 4–5 minutes until the mussels have opened.

3 Drain the mussels, reserving all the juices. Discard any mussels that remain closed.

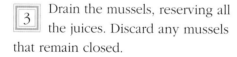

4 Melt the butter in a large clean pan and gently fry the fennel slices and garlic for about 5 minutes until softened.

5 Stir in the curry paste or powder and flour and cook for 1 minute. Remove from the heat and gradually blend in the cooking juices from the mussels. Return to the heat and cook, stirring, for 2 minutes.

6 Stir in the cream and a little pepper. Add the mussels to the pan and heat through for 2 minutes. Serve hot, garnished with dill.

VARIATION
Saffron is a popular addition to a mouclade. Soak 2.5ml/½ tsp saffron strands in a little boiling water and add to the sauce with the stock.

OCTOPUS AND RED WINE STEW

Unless you're happy to clean and prepare octopus for this Greek dish, buy one that's ready for cooking.

900g/2lb prepared octopus
450g/1lb onions, sliced
2 bay leaves
450g/1lb ripe tomatoes
60ml/4 tbsp olive oil
4 garlic cloves, crushed
5ml/1 tsp caster sugar
15ml/1 tbsp chopped fresh oregano
or rosemary
30ml/2 tbsp chopped fresh parsley
150ml/¼ pint/⅔ cup red wine
30ml/2 tbsp red wine vinegar
chopped fresh herbs, to garnish
warm bread and pine nuts, to serve

SERVES 4

1 Put the octopus in a saucepan of gently simmering water with a quarter of the onions and the bay leaves. Cook gently for 1 hour.

2 While the octopus is cooking, plunge the tomatoes into boiling water for 30 seconds, then refresh in cold water. Peel away the skins and chop roughly.

3 Drain the octopus and, using a sharp knife, cut it into bite-size pieces. Discard the head.

4 Heat the oil in a saucepan and fry the octopus, the remaining onions and the garlic for 3 minutes. Add the tomatoes, sugar, oregano or rosemary, parsley, wine and vinegar and cook, stirring, for 5 minutes until pulpy.

5 Cover the pan and cook over the lowest possible heat for about 1½ hours until the sauce is thickened and the octopus is tender. Garnish with fresh herbs and serve with plenty of warm bread, and pine nuts to scatter on top.

FRESH TUNA AND TOMATO STEW

A deliciously simple dish that relies on good basic ingredients. For real Italian flavour serve with polenta or pasta.

12 baby onions, peeled
900g/2lb ripe tomatoes
675g/1½lb fresh tuna
45ml/3 tbsp olive oil
2 garlic cloves, crushed
45ml/3 tbsp chopped fresh herbs
2 bay leaves
2.5ml/½ tsp caster sugar
30ml/2 tbsp sun-dried tomato paste
150ml/¼ pint/⅔ cup dry white wine
salt and ground black pepper
baby courgettes and fresh herbs,
to garnish

SERVES 4

VARIATION

Two large mackerel make a more readily available alternative to the tuna. Fillet them and cut into chunks or simply lay the whole fish over the sauce and cook, covered with a lid until the mackerel is cooked through. Sage, rosemary or oregano all go extremely well with this dish. Choose whichever you prefer, or use a mixture of one or two.

[1] Leave the onions whole and cook in a pan of boiling water for 4–5 minutes until softened. Drain.

[2] Plunge the tomatoes into boiling water for 30 seconds, then refresh in cold water. Peel away the skins and chop roughly.

[3] Cut the tuna into 2.5cm/1in chunks. Heat the oil in a large frying or sauté pan and quickly fry the tuna until browned. Drain.

[4] Add the onions, garlic, tomatoes, chopped herbs, bay leaves, sugar, tomato paste and wine and bring to the boil, breaking up the tomatoes with a wooden spoon.

[5] Reduce the heat and simmer gently for 5 minutes. Return the fish to the pan and cook for a further 5 minutes. Season, and serve hot, garnished with baby courgettes and fresh herbs.

BRODETTO

The different regions of Italy have their own variations of this dish, but all require a good fish stock.
Make sure you buy some of the fish whole so you can simply simmer them, remove the cooked flesh and
strain the deliciously flavoured juices to make the stock.

900g/2lb mixture of fish fillets or
steaks, such as monkfish, cod,
haddock, halibut or hake
900g/2lb mixture of conger eel, red or
grey mullet, snapper or small
white fish
1 onion, halved
1 celery stick, roughly chopped
225g/8oz squid
225g/8oz fresh mussels
675g/1½lb ripe tomatoes
60ml/4 tbsp olive oil
1 large onion, thinly sliced
3 garlic cloves, crushed
5ml/1 tsp saffron strands
150ml/¼ pint/⅔ cup dry white wine
90ml/6 tbsp chopped fresh parsley
salt and ground black pepper
croûtons, to serve

SERVES 4–5

1 Remove any skin and bones from the fish fillets or steaks, cut the fish into large pieces and reserve. Place the bones in a pan with all the remaining fish.

2 Add the halved onion and the celery and just cover with water. Bring almost to the boil, then reduce the heat and simmer gently for about 30 minutes. Lift out the fish and remove the flesh from the bones. Reserve the stock.

3 To prepare the squid, twist the head and tentacles away from the body. Cut the head from the tentacles. Discard the body contents and peel away the mottled skin. Wash the tentacles and bodies and dry on kitchen paper.

COOK'S TIP
To make the croûtons, cut thin slices from a long thin stick of bread and shallow fry in a little butter until golden.

4 Scrub the mussels, discarding any that are damaged or open ones that do not close when tapped.

5 Plunge the tomatoes into boiling water for 30 seconds, then refresh in cold water. Peel away the skins and chop roughly.

6 Heat the oil in a large saucepan or sauté pan. Add the sliced onion and the garlic and fry gently for 3 minutes. Add the squid and the uncooked white fish, which you reserved earlier, and fry quickly on all sides. Drain.

7 Add 475ml/16fl oz/2 cups strained reserved fish stock, the saffron and tomatoes to the pan. Pour in the wine. Bring to the boil, then reduce the heat and simmer for about 5 minutes. Add the mussels, cover, and cook for 3–4 minutes until the mussels have opened. Discard any that remain closed.

8 Season the sauce with salt and pepper and put all the fish in the pan. Cook gently for 5 minutes. Scatter with the parsley and serve with the croûtons.

SARDINE GRATIN

In Sicily and other countries in the Western Mediterranean, sardines are filled with a robust stuffing, flavoursome enough to compete with the rich oiliness of the fish itself.

15ml/1 tbsp light olive oil
½ small onion, finely chopped
2 garlic cloves, crushed
40g/1½oz/6 tbsp blanched
almonds, chopped
25g/1oz/2 tbsp sultanas,
roughly chopped
10 pitted black olives
30ml/2 tbsp capers, roughly chopped
30ml/2 tbsp roughly chopped
fresh parsley
50g/2oz/1 cup breadcrumbs
16 large sardines, scaled and gutted
25g/1oz/⅓ cup grated
Parmesan cheese
salt and ground black pepper
flat leaf parsley, to garnish

SERVES 4

1 Preheat the oven to 200°C/
400°F/Gas 6. Lightly oil a large
shallow ovenproof dish.

2 Heat the oil in a frying pan and
fry the onion and garlic gently
for 3 minutes. Stir in the almonds,
sultanas, olives, capers, parsley and
25g/1oz/¼ cup of the breadcrumbs.
Season lightly with salt and pepper.

*ABOVE: Brodetto (top) and Sardine
Gratin (bottom).*

3 Make 2–3 diagonal cuts on each
side of the sardines. Pack the
stuffing into the cavities and lay the
sardines in the prepared dish.

4 Mix the remaining breadcrumbs
with the cheese and scatter over
the fish. Bake for about 20 minutes
until the fish is cooked through. Test
by piercing one sardine through the
thickest part with a knife. Garnish
with parsley and serve immediately
with a leafy salad.

ZARZUELA

Zarzuela means "light opera" or "musical comedy" in Spanish and the classic fish stew of the same name should be as lively and colourful as the zarzuela itself. This feast of fish includes lobster and other shellfish, but you can modify the ingredients to suit the occasion and availability.

1 cooked lobster
24 fresh mussels or clams
1 large monkfish tail
225g/8oz squid rings
15ml/1 tbsp plain flour
90ml/6 tbsp olive oil
12 large raw prawns
450g/1lb ripe tomatoes
2 large mild onions, chopped
4 garlic cloves, crushed
30ml/2 tbsp brandy
2 bay leaves
5ml/1 tsp paprika
1 red chilli, seeded and chopped
300ml/½ pint/1¼ cups fish stock
15g/½oz/2 tbsp ground almonds
30ml/2 tbsp chopped fresh parsley
salt and ground black pepper

SERVES 6

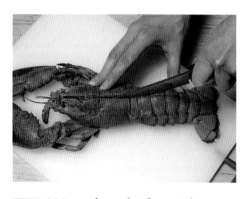

1 Using a large knife, cut the lobster in half lengthways. Remove the dark intestine that runs down the length of the tail. Crack the claws using a hammer.

2 Scrub the mussels, discarding any that are damaged or open ones that do not close when tapped with a knife. Cut the monkfish fillets away from the central cartilage and cut each fillet into three.

3 Toss the monkfish and squid in seasoned flour. Heat the oil in a large frying pan. Add the monkfish and squid and fry quickly; remove from the pan. Fry the prawns on both sides, then remove from the pan.

4 Plunge the tomatoes into boiling water for 30 seconds, then refresh in cold water. Peel away the skins and chop roughly.

5 Add the onions and two-thirds of the garlic to the frying pan and fry for 3 minutes. Add the brandy and ignite with a taper. When the flames die down, add the tomatoes, bay leaves, paprika, chilli and stock.

6 Bring to the boil, reduce the heat and simmer gently for 5 minutes. Add the mussels or clams, cover and cook for 3–4 minutes, until the shells have opened.

7 Remove the mussels or clams from the sauce and discard any that remain closed.

8 Arrange all the fish, including the lobster, in a large flameproof serving dish. Blend the ground almonds to a paste with the remaining garlic and parsley and stir into the sauce. Season with salt and pepper.

9 Pour the sauce over the fish and lobster and cook gently for about 5 minutes until hot. Serve immediately with a green salad and plenty of warmed bread.

BAKED FISH WITH TAHINI SAUCE

This North African recipe evokes all the colour and rich flavours of Mediterranean cuisine. Choose any whole white fish, such as sea bass, hake, bream or snapper.

1 whole fish, about 1.1kg/2½lb, scaled and cleaned
10ml/2 tsp coriander seeds
4 garlic cloves, sliced
10ml/2 tsp harissa sauce
90ml/6 tbsp olive oil
6 plum tomatoes, sliced
1 mild onion, sliced
3 preserved lemons or 1 fresh lemon
plenty of fresh herbs, such as bay leaves, thyme and rosemary
salt and ground black pepper

FOR THE SAUCE
75ml/3fl oz/⅓ cup light tahini
juice of 1 lemon
1 garlic clove, crushed
45ml/3 tbsp finely chopped fresh parsley or coriander
extra herbs, to garnish

SERVES 4

1 Preheat the oven to 200°C/ 400°F/Gas 6. Grease the base and sides of a large shallow ovenproof dish or roasting tin.

2 Slash the fish diagonally on both sides with a sharp knife. Finely crush the coriander seeds and garlic with a pestle and mortar. Mix with the harissa sauce and about 60ml/4 tbsp of the olive oil.

3 Spread a little of the harissa, coriander and garlic paste inside the cavity of the fish. Spread the remainder over each side of the fish and set aside.

4 Scatter the tomatoes, onion and preserved or fresh lemon into the dish. (Thinly slice the lemon if using fresh.) Sprinkle with the remaining oil and season with salt and pepper. Lay the fish on top and tuck plenty of herbs around it.

5 Bake, uncovered, for about 25 minutes, or until the fish has turned opaque – test by piercing the thickest part with a knife.

6 Meanwhile, make the sauce. Put the tahini, lemon juice, garlic and parsley or coriander in a small saucepan with 120ml/4fl oz/½ cup water and add a little salt and pepper. Cook gently until smooth and heated through. Serve in a separate dish.

COOK'S TIP
If you can't get a suitable large fish, use small whole fish such as red mullet or even cod or haddock steaks. Remember to reduce the cooking time slightly.

STUFFED SQUID

This Greek delicacy is best made with large squid as they are less fiddly to stuff. If you have to make do with small squid, buy about 450g/1lb.

FOR THE STUFFING
30ml/2 tbsp olive oil
1 large onion, finely chopped
2 garlic cloves, crushed
50g/2oz/1 cup fresh breadcrumbs
60ml/4 tbsp chopped fresh parsley
115g/4oz halloumi cheese, grated
salt and ground black pepper

TO FINISH
4 squid tubes, each about
18cm/7in long
900g/2lb ripe tomatoes
45ml/3 tbsp olive oil
1 large onion, chopped
5ml/1 tsp caster sugar
120ml/4fl oz/½ cup dry white wine
several rosemary sprigs
toasted pine nuts and flat leaf parsley,
to garnish

SERVES 4

1 To make the stuffing, heat the oil in a frying pan and fry the onion for 3 minutes. Remove the pan from the heat and add the garlic, breadcrumbs, parsley, cheese and a little salt and pepper. Stir until thoroughly blended.

2 Dry the squid tubes on kitchen paper and fill with the prepared stuffing using a teaspoon. Secure the ends of the squid tubes with wooden cocktail sticks.

VARIATION
If you would prefer a less rich filling, halve the quantity of cheese and breadcrumbs in the stuffing and add 225g/8oz cooked spinach.

3 Plunge the tomatoes into boiling water for 30 seconds, then refresh in cold water. Peel away the skins and chop roughly.

4 Heat the oil in a frying pan or sauté pan. Add the squid and fry on all sides. Remove from the pan.

5 Add the onion to the pan and fry gently for 3 minutes. Stir in the tomatoes, sugar and wine and cook rapidly until the mixture becomes thick and pulpy.

6 Return the squid to the pan with the rosemary. Cover and cook gently for 30 minutes. Slice the squid and serve on individual plates with the sauce. Scatter over the pine nuts and garnish with parsley.

HAKE AND CLAMS WITH SALSA VERDE

Hake is one of the most popular fish in Spain and here it is cooked in a sauce flavoured with parsley, lemon juice and garlic.

4 hake steaks, about 2cm/¾in thick
50g/2oz/½ cup plain flour for dusting, plus 30ml/2 tbsp
60ml/4 tbsp olive oil
15ml/1 tbsp lemon juice
1 small onion, finely chopped
4 garlic cloves, crushed
150ml/¼ pint/⅔ cup fish stock
150ml/¼ pint/⅔ cup white wine
90ml/6 tbsp chopped fresh parsley
75g/3oz frozen petits pois
16 fresh clams
salt and ground black pepper

SERVES 4

 1 Preheat the oven to 180°C/ 350°F/Gas 4. Season the fish with salt and pepper, then dust both sides with flour. Heat 30ml/2 tbsp of the oil in a large sauté pan, add the fish and fry for about 1 minute on each side. Transfer to an ovenproof dish and sprinkle with lemon juice.

2 Clean the pan, then heat the remaining oil. Add the onion and garlic and cook until soft. Stir in 30ml/2 tbsp flour and cook for about 1 minute. Gradually add the stock and wine, stirring until thickened and smooth. Add 75ml/5 tbsp of the parsley and the petits pois and season with salt and pepper.

3 Pour the sauce over the fish, and bake in the oven for 15–20 minutes, adding the clams to the dish 3–4 minutes before the end of the cooking time. Discard any clams that do not open, then sprinkle with the remaining parsley before serving.

COD PLAKI

Greece has so much coastline, it's no wonder that fish is popular all over the country. Generally, it is treated very simply, but this recipe is a little more involved, baking the fish with onions and tomatoes.

300ml/½ pint/1¼ cups olive oil
2 onions, thinly sliced
3 large well-flavoured tomatoes,
roughly chopped
3 garlic cloves, thinly sliced
5ml/1 tsp sugar
5ml/1 tsp chopped fresh dill
5ml/1 tsp chopped fresh mint
5ml/1 tsp chopped fresh celery leaves
15ml/1 tbsp chopped fresh parsley
6 cod steaks
juice of 1 lemon
salt and ground black pepper
extra dill, mint or parsley, to garnish

SERVES 6

1 Heat the oil in a large sauté pan or flameproof dish. Add the onions and cook until pale golden. Add the tomatoes, garlic, sugar, dill, mint, celery leaves and parsley with 300ml/½ pint/1¼ cups water. Season with salt and pepper, then simmer, uncovered, for 25 minutes, until the liquid has reduced by one-third.

2 Add the fish steaks and cook gently for 10–12 minutes, until the fish is just cooked. Remove from the heat and add the lemon juice (*left*). Cover and leave to stand for about 20 minutes before serving. Arrange the cod in a dish and spoon the sauce over. Garnish with herbs and serve warm or cold.

MEAT

*The Mediterranean style of cooking makes the
most of young lamb and pork, while tougher cuts
are slow-cooked in superb sauces.*

Unlike the vegetable and fish dishes of the Mediterranean, meat recipes do not spring to mind very readily. The countryside around the Mediterranean can be quite harsh – no lush, green fields for animals to graze. Beasts are often slaughtered young, and baby lamb and goat are favourite meats. These animals were usually roasted whole on a spit, flavoured with wild herbs, and eaten on feast days. The meat of the young kid is particularly popular in the less sophisticated parts of the Mediterranean, such as Corsica, parts of Greece and the Middle East. Cattle are a rare sight and, in times past, beef was considered a luxury. Many rural families kept a pig, which was slaughtered and the meat was preserved, to feed them through the chilly winter months. This, in turn, inspired the many wonderful dry sausages, like salami, and the cured hams, which are still popular today, and appreciated all over the world. Both Jews and Muslims were forbidden by their religion to eat pork so there are no traditional pork recipes from their countries

ABOVE: Sunlight dapples the walls of this farmhouse overlooking Lake Trasimeno, in Umbria.

and regions. In the Middle East, only lamb and mutton were eaten, although nowadays beef and veal are becoming more popular. The Roman Catholic and Greek Orthodox Churches used to have strict rules concerning "lean" days, when meat could not be consumed, and therefore many special feast dishes using meat were created to celebrate the end of these regular fasts.

Meat was often of poor quality, if the beast had not been properly fed, and this resulted in tough and stringy cuts. This was remedied by marinating the meat in wine or yogurt, cooking it slowly at a low temperature, to tenderize it and improve the flavour. These methods resulted in some of the most delicious recipes for casseroles and stews. Many are still cooked today, despite the fact that the meat is probably of better quality. *Daubes* from France, *tagines* from Morocco, *estofados*

RIGHT: *This French shepherd has a magnificent view of the Provençal countryside.*

BELOW: *Sacks of spices and grains invite inspection at a Tunisian market.*

from Spain; every country has its own version, recipes having been handed down through the generations. As meat was a luxury, pulses, rice and potatoes were often added to the pot, to make the meal go further.

Another popular method of cooking meat is grilling. Quite often the meat is threaded on to skewers, or sometimes a branch of rosemary or bay, with chunks of onion and other vegetables. This is a basic form of cooking, originating from the need to cook over the hot embers of an open fire, and results in succulent, smoky-flavoured meat. Greece and the Middle East have mastered this technique, and the smell of meat cooking on a wood fire is one associated with these countries. Using minced

meat, in the form of patties, meatballs, sausages, sauces for pasta and fillings for savoury pastries is popular throughout the Mediterranean. This was another way of padding out meat with other ingredients to make a more economical dish. Breadcrumbs, rice, bulgur and potatoes are all used to add more bulk, particularly when making meatballs and patties. Onion and tomatoes give flavour and volume to sauces. In the Middle East, spices, nuts and dried fruits are often mixed with minced meat, to make delicious fillings for little parcels of filo. Elsewhere, in Italy, garlic, wine, and herbs are added to slow-cooked meat sauces, to eat with pasta. In Greece, minced lamb is layered with aubergines, tomato sauce, and béchamel sauce to create Moussaka, and in Turkey, minced lamb is used to stuff halved aubergines, the vegetable flesh being mixed with the minced meat. These versatile dishes are good for feeding a large crowd, often making a little go a long way.

Although there are no recipes for goat in this chapter (as it is not readily available), the selection varies from Corsican Beef with Macaroni to Turkish Lamb Pilau and Greek Lamb Sausages with Tomato Sauce. As with most recipes in this book, all that is needed to accompany any of them, once cooked and ready to eat, is a glass of wine (in this case red) and some good bread!

TURKISH LAMB PILAU

a delicious combination of rice, lamb, spices, nuts and fruit — a typical
Middle Eastern dish.

40g/1½oz/3 tbsp butter
1 large onion, finely chopped
450g/1lb lamb fillet, cut into
small cubes
2.5ml/½ tsp ground cinnamon
30ml/2 tbsp tomato purée
45ml/3 tbsp chopped fresh parsley
115g/4oz/½ cup ready-to-eat dried
apricots, halved
75g/3oz/¾ cup pistachio nuts
450g/1lb long grain rice, rinsed
salt and ground black pepper
flat leaf parsley, to garnish

SERVES 4

1 Heat the butter in a large heavy-based pan. Add the onion and cook until soft and golden. Add the cubed lamb and brown on all sides. Add the cinnamon and season with salt and pepper. Cover and cook gently for 10 minutes.

2 Add the tomato purée and enough water to cover the meat. Stir in the parsley, bring to the boil, cover and simmer very gently for 1½ hours, until the meat is tender. Chop the pistachio nuts.

3 Add enough water to the pan to make up to about 600ml/1 pint/2½ cups liquid. Add the apricots, pistachio nuts and rice, bring to the boil, cover tightly and simmer for about 20 minutes, until the rice is cooked. (You may need to add a little more water, if necessary.) Transfer to a warmed serving dish and garnish with parsley before serving.

GREEK LAMB SAUSAGES WITH TOMATO SAUCE

The Greek name for these sausages is soudzoukakia. They are more like elongated meatballs than the type of sausage we are accustomed to. Passata is sieved tomato, which can be bought in cartons or jars.

50g/2oz/1 cup fresh breadcrumbs
150ml/¼ pint/⅔ cup milk
675g/1½lb minced lamb
30ml/2 tbsp grated onion
3 garlic cloves, crushed
10ml/2 tsp ground cumin
30ml/2 tbsp chopped fresh parsley
flour for dusting
olive oil for frying
600ml/1 pint/2½ cups passata
5ml/1 tsp sugar
2 bay leaves
1 small onion, peeled
salt and ground black pepper
flat leaf parsley, to garnish

SERVES 4

1. Mix together the breadcrumbs and milk. Add the lamb, onion, garlic, cumin and parsley and season with salt and pepper.

2. Shape the mixture with your hands into little fat sausages, about 5cm/2in long and roll them in flour. Heat about 60ml/4 tbsp olive oil in a frying pan.

3. Fry the sausages for about 8 minutes, turning them until evenly browned. Remove and place on kitchen paper to drain.

4. Put the passata, sugar, bay leaves and whole onion in a pan and simmer for 20 minutes. Add the sausages and cook for 10 minutes more. Serve garnished with parsley.

ROAST LOIN OF PORK STUFFED WITH FIGS, OLIVES AND ALMONDS

Pork is a popular meat in Spain, and this recipe using fruit and nuts in the stuffing is of Catalan influence, where the combination of meat and fruit is quite common.

2 Remove any string from the pork and unroll the belly flap, cutting away any excess fat or meat, to enable you to do so. Spread half the stuffing over the flat piece and roll up, starting from the thick side. Tie at intervals with string.

3 Pour the remaining oil into a small roasting tin and put in the pork. Roast for 1 hour 15 minutes. Form the remaining stuffing mixture into balls and add to the roasting tin around the meat, 15–20 minutes before the end of cooking time.

60ml/4 tbsp olive oil
1 onion, finely chopped
2 garlic cloves, chopped
75g/3oz/1½ cups fresh breadcrumbs
4 ready-to-eat dried figs, chopped
8 pitted green olives, chopped
25g/1oz/¼ cup flaked almonds
15ml/1 tbsp lemon juice
15ml/1 tbsp chopped fresh parsley
1 egg yolk
900g/2lb boned loin of pork
salt and ground black pepper

SERVES 4

1 Preheat the oven to 200°C/ 400°F/Gas 6. Heat 45ml/3 tbsp of the oil in a pan, add the onion and garlic, and cook gently until softened. Remove the pan from the heat and stir in the breadcrumbs, figs, olives, almonds, lemon juice, parsley and egg yolk. Season to taste.

COOK'S TIP
Keep a tub of breadcrumbs in the freezer. They can be used frozen.

4 Remove the pork from the oven and let it rest for 10 minutes. Carve into thick slices and serve with the stuffing balls and any juices from the tin. This is also good served cold.

142

LAMB WITH RED PEPPERS AND RIOJA

Plenty of garlic, peppers, herbs and red wine give this lamb stew a lovely rich flavour.
Slice through the pepper stalks, rather than removing them, as this makes it look
extra special.

900g/2lb lean lamb fillet
15ml/1 tbsp plain flour
60ml/4 tbsp olive oil
2 red onions, sliced
4 garlic cloves, sliced
10ml/2 tsp paprika
1.5ml/¼ tsp ground cloves
400ml/14fl oz/1⅔ cups red Rioja
150ml/¼ pint/⅔ cup lamb stock
2 bay leaves
2 thyme sprigs
3 red peppers, halved and seeded
salt and ground black pepper
bay leaves and thyme sprigs,
to garnish
green beans and saffron rice or boiled
potatoes, to serve

SERVES 4

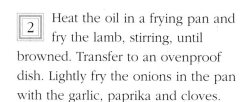

1 Preheat the oven to 160°C/ 325°F/Gas 3. Cut the lamb into chunks. Season the flour, add the lamb and toss lightly to coat.

2 Heat the oil in a frying pan and fry the lamb, stirring, until browned. Transfer to an ovenproof dish. Lightly fry the onions in the pan with the garlic, paprika and cloves.

VARIATION
Use any lean cubed pork instead of the lamb and a white Rioja instead of the red. A mixture of red, yellow and orange peppers looks very effective.

3 Add the Rioja, stock, bay leaves and thyme and bring to the boil, stirring. Pour the contents of the pan over the meat. Cover with a lid and bake for 30 minutes.

4 Remove the dish from the oven. Stir the red peppers into the stew and season lightly with salt and pepper. Bake for a further 30 minutes until the meat is tender. Garnish the stew with bay leaves and sprigs of thyme and serve with green beans and saffron rice or boiled potatoes.

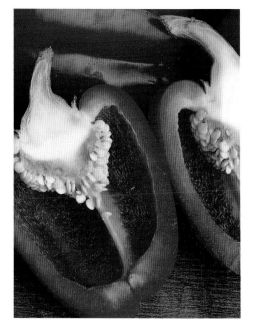

CORSICAN BEEF STEW WITH MACARONI

Pasta is eaten in many parts of the Mediterranean. In Corsica, it's often served with gravy as a sauce and, in this case, a rich beef stew.

25g/1oz dried mushrooms (ceps or porcini)
6 garlic cloves
900g/2lb stewing beef, cut into 5cm/2in cubes
115g/4oz lardons, or thick streaky bacon cut into strips
45ml/3 tbsp olive oil
2 onions, sliced
300ml/½ pint/1¼ cups dry white wine
30ml/2 tbsp passata
pinch of ground cinnamon
sprig of rosemary
1 bay leaf
225g/8oz/2 cups large macaroni
50g/2oz/⅔ cup freshly grated Parmesan cheese
salt and ground black pepper

SERVES 4

1 Soak the dried mushrooms in warm water for 30 minutes. Drain, set the mushrooms aside and reserve the liquid. Cut three of the garlic cloves into thin strips and insert into the pieces of beef by making little slits with a sharp knife. Push the lardons or pieces of bacon into the beef with the garlic. Season the meat with salt and pepper.

3 Stir in the white wine, passata, mushrooms, cinnamon, rosemary and bay leaf and season with salt and pepper. Cook gently for 30 minutes, stirring often. Strain the mushroom liquid and add to the stew with enough water to cover. Bring to the boil, cover and simmer very gently for 3 hours, until the meat is very tender.

2 Heat the oil in a heavy-based pan, add half the beef and brown well on all sides. Repeat with the remaining beef. Transfer to a plate. Add the sliced onions to the pan and cook until lightly browned. Crush the remaining garlic and add to the onions with the meat.

4 Cook the macaroni in a large pan of boiling, salted water for 10 minutes, or until *al dente*. Lift the pieces of meat out of the gravy and transfer to a warmed serving platter. Drain the pasta and layer in a serving bowl with the gravy and cheese. Serve with the meat.

AFELIA

This lightly-spiced pork stew makes a really delicious supper dish served simply, as it would be in Cyprus, with warmed bread, a leafy salad and a few olives.

3 Preheat the oven to 160°C/325°F/Gas 3. Heat 30ml/2 tbsp of the oil in a frying pan over a high heat. Brown the meat quickly, then transfer to an ovenproof dish.

675g/1½lb pork fillet, boneless leg or chump steaks
20ml/4 tsp coriander seeds
2.5ml/½ tsp caster sugar
45ml/3 tbsp olive oil
2 large onions, sliced
300ml/½ pint/1¼ cups red wine
salt and ground black pepper
fresh coriander, to garnish

SERVES 4

COOK'S TIP
A coffee grinder can also be used to grind the coriander seeds. Alternatively, use 15ml/1 tbsp ground coriander.

1 Cut the pork into small chunks, discarding any excess fat. Crush the coriander seeds with a pestle and mortar until fairly finely ground.

2 Mix the coriander seeds with the sugar and salt and pepper and rub all over the meat. Leave to marinate for up to 4 hours.

4 Add the remaining oil to the pan and fry the onions until beginning to colour. Stir in the wine and a little salt and pepper and bring just to the boil.

5 Pour the onion and wine mixture over the meat and cover with a lid. Bake for 1 hour, or until the meat is very tender. Serve scattered with fresh coriander.

MOUSSAKA

...ular classics, a real moussaka bears little resemblance to the imitations experienced in ...urist resorts. This one is mildly spiced, moist but not dripping in grease, and encased in a golden baked crust.

900g/2lb aubergines
120ml/4fl oz/½ cup olive oil
2 large tomatoes
2 large onions, sliced
450g/1lb minced lamb
1.5ml/¼ tsp ground cinnamon
1.5ml/¼ tsp ground allspice
30ml/2 tbsp tomato purée
45ml/3 tbsp chopped fresh parsley
120ml/4fl oz/½ cup dry white wine
salt and ground black pepper

FOR THE SAUCE
50g/2oz/4 tbsp butter
50g/2oz/½ cup plain flour
600ml/1 pint/2½ cups milk
1.5ml/¼ tsp grated nutmeg
25g/1oz/⅓ cup grated
Parmesan cheese
45ml/3 tbsp toasted breadcrumbs

SERVES 6

1 Cut the aubergines into 5mm/¼in thick slices. Layer the slices in a colander, sprinkling each layer with plenty of salt. Leave to stand for 30 minutes.

2 Rinse the aubergines in several changes of cold water. Squeeze gently with your fingers to remove the excess water, then pat them dry on kitchen paper.

3 Heat some of the oil in a large frying pan. Fry the aubergine slices in batches until golden on both sides, adding more oil when necessary. Leave the fried aubergine slices to drain on kitchen paper.

4 Plunge the tomatoes into boiling water for 30 seconds, then refresh in cold water. Peel away the skins and chop roughly.

5 Preheat the oven to 180°C/350°F/Gas 4. Heat 30ml/2 tbsp oil in a saucepan. Add the onions and lamb and fry gently for 5 minutes, stirring and breaking up the lamb with a wooden spoon.

VARIATION
Sliced and sautéed courgettes or potatoes can be used instead of the aubergines in this dish.

6 Add the tomatoes, cinnamon, allspice, tomato purée, parsley, wine and pepper and bring to the boil. Reduce the heat, cover with a lid and simmer gently for 15 minutes.

7 Spoon alternate layers of the aubergines and meat mixture into a shallow ovenproof dish, finishing with a layer of aubergines.

8 To make the sauce, melt the butter in a small pan and stir in the flour. Cook, stirring, for 1 minute. Remove from the heat and gradually blend in the milk. Return to the heat and cook, stirring, for 2 minutes, until thickened. Add the nutmeg, cheese and salt and pepper. Pour the sauce over the aubergines and sprinkle with the breadcrumbs. Bake for 45 minutes until golden. Serve hot, sprinkled with extra black pepper, if you like.

BEEF ROLLS WITH GARLIC AND TOMATO SAUCE

Italy has many regional variations on the technique of wrapping thin slices of beef around a richly flavoured stuffing. This recipe incorporates some of the classic ingredients.

4 thin slices of rump steak, (about 115g/4oz each)
4 slices smoked ham
150g/5oz Pecorini cheese, grated
2 garlic cloves, crushed
75ml/5 tbsp chopped fresh parsley
2 eggs, soft-boiled and shelled
45ml/3 tbsp olive oil
1 large onion, finely chopped
150ml/¼ pint/⅔ cup passata
75ml/3fl oz/⅓ cup red wine
2 bay leaves
150ml/¼ pint/⅔ cup beef stock
salt and ground black pepper
flat leaf parsley, to garnish

SERVES 4

1 Preheat the oven to 160°C/325°F/Gas 3. Lay the beef slices on a sheet of greaseproof paper. Cover the beef with another sheet of greaseproof paper or clear film and beat with a mallet or rolling pin until very thin.

2 Lay a ham slice over each. Mix the cheese in a bowl with the garlic, parsley, eggs and a little salt and pepper. Stir well until all the ingredients are evenly mixed.

3 Spoon the stuffing on to the ham and beef slices. Fold two opposite sides of the meat over the stuffing, then roll up the meat to form neat parcels. Secure with string.

4 Heat the oil in a frying pan. Add the parcels and fry quickly on all sides to brown. Transfer to an ovenproof dish.

5 Add the onion to the frying pan and fry for 3 minutes. Stir in the passata, wine, bay leaves and stock and season with salt and pepper. Bring to the boil, then pour the sauce over the meat in the dish.

6 Cover the dish and bake in the oven for 1 hour. Drain the meat and remove the string. Spoon on to warmed serving plates. Taste the sauce, adding extra salt and pepper if necessary, and spoon it over the meat. Serve garnished with flat leaf parsley.

PORK WITH MARSALA AND JUNIPER

Although most frequently used in desserts, Sicilian marsala gives savoury dishes a rich, fruity and alcoholic tang. Use good quality butcher's pork which won't be drowned by the flavour of the sauce.

25g/1oz dried cep or porcini mushrooms
4 pork escalopes
10ml/2 tsp balsamic vinegar
8 garlic cloves
15g/½oz/1 tbsp butter
45ml/3 tbsp marsala
several rosemary sprigs
10 juniper berries, crushed
salt and ground black pepper
noodles and green vegetables, to serve

SERVES 4

1 Put the dried mushrooms in a bowl and just cover with hot water. Leave to stand.

2 Brush the pork with 5ml/1 tsp of the vinegar and season with salt and pepper. Put the garlic cloves in a small pan of boiling water and cook for 10 minutes until soft. Drain and set aside.

3 Melt the butter in a large frying pan. Add the pork and fry quickly until browned on the underside. Turn the meat over and cook for another minute.

4 Add the marsala, rosemary, mushrooms, 60ml/4 tbsp of the mushroom juices, the garlic cloves, juniper and remaining vinegar.

5 Simmer gently for about 3 minutes until the pork is cooked through. Season lightly and serve hot with noodles and green vegetables.

SKEWERED LAMB WITH CORIANDER YOGURT

Although lamb is the most commonly used meat for Turkish kebabs, lean beef or pork work equally well.
For colour you can alternate pieces of pepper, lemon or onions, although this is not traditional.

900g/2lb lean boneless lamb
1 large onion, grated
3 bay leaves
5 thyme or rosemary sprigs
grated rind and juice of
1 lemon
2.5ml/½ tsp caster sugar
75ml/3fl oz/⅓ cup olive oil
salt and ground black pepper
sprigs of rosemary, to garnish
grilled lemon wedges, to serve

FOR THE CORIANDER YOGURT
150ml/¼ pint/⅔ cup thick
natural yogurt
15ml/1 tbsp chopped fresh mint
15ml/1 tbsp chopped fresh coriander
10ml/2 tsp grated onion

SERVES 4

1 To make the coriander yogurt, mix together the yogurt, mint, coriander and grated onion and transfer to a small serving dish.

2 To make the kebabs, cut the lamb into small chunks and put in a bowl. Mix together the grated onion, herbs, lemon rind and juice, sugar and oil, then add salt and pepper and pour over the lamb.

3 Mix the ingredients together and leave to marinate in the fridge for several hours or overnight.

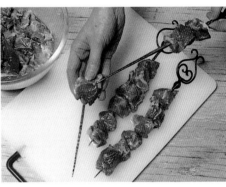

4 Drain the meat and thread on to skewers. Arrange on a grill rack and cook under a preheated grill for about 10 minutes until browned, turning occasionally. Transfer to a plate and garnish with rosemary. Serve with the grilled lemon wedges and the coriander yogurt.

COOK'S TIP
Cover the tips of wooden skewers with foil so they don't char.

KLEFTIKO

For this Greek recipe, marinated lamb steaks or chops are slow-cooked to develop an unbeatable, meltingly tender flavour. The dish is sealed, like a pie, with a flour dough lid to trap succulence and flavour, although a tight-fitting foil cover, if less attractive, will serve equally well.

juice of 1 lemon
15ml/1 tbsp chopped fresh oregano
4 lamb leg steaks or chump chops
with bones
30ml/2 tbsp olive oil
2 large onions, thinly sliced
2 bay leaves
150ml/¼ pint/⅔ cup dry white wine
225g/8oz/2 cups plain flour
salt and ground black pepper

SERVES 4

COOK'S TIP
They are not absolutely essential for this dish, but lamb steaks or chops with bones will provide lots of additional flavour. Boiled potatoes make a delicious accompaniment.

1 Mix together the lemon juice, oregano and salt and pepper, and brush over both sides of the lamb steaks or chops. Leave to marinate for at least 4 hours or overnight.

2 Preheat the oven to 160°C/ 325°F/Gas 3. Drain the lamb, reserving the marinade, and dry the lamb with kitchen paper. Heat the olive oil in a large frying pan or sauté pan and fry the lamb over a high heat until browned on both sides.

3 Transfer the lamb to a shallow pie dish. Scatter the sliced onions and bay leaves around the lamb, then pour over the white wine and the reserved marinade.

4 Mix the flour with sufficient water to make a firm dough. Moisten the rim of the pie dish. Roll out the dough on a floured surface and use to cover the dish so that it is tightly sealed.

5 Bake for 2 hours, then break away the dough crust and serve the lamb hot with boiled potatoes.

BLACK BEAN STEW

This simple Spanish stew uses a few robust ingredients to create a deliciously intense flavour, rather like a French cassoulet.

275g/10oz/1⅓ cups black beans
675g/1½lb boneless belly pork rashers
60ml/4 tbsp olive oil
350g/12oz baby onions
2 celery sticks, thickly sliced
10ml/2 tsp paprika
150g/5oz chorizo sausage, cut
into chunks
600ml/1 pint/2½ cups light chicken or
vegetable stock
2 green peppers, seeded and cut into
large pieces
salt and ground black pepper

SERVES 5–6

1 Put the beans in a bowl and cover with plenty of cold water. Leave to soak overnight. Drain the beans into a saucepan and cover with fresh water. Bring to the boil and boil rapidly for 10 minutes. Drain.

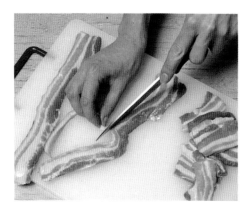

2 Preheat the oven to 160°C/325°F/Gas 3. Cut away any rind from the pork and cut the meat into large chunks.

3 Heat the oil in a large frying pan and fry the onions and celery for 3 minutes. Add the pork and fry for 5–10 minutes until the pork is browned.

4 Add the paprika and chorizo and fry for a further 2 minutes. Transfer to an ovenproof dish with the beans and mix together.

5 Add the stock to the pan and bring to the boil. Season lightly, then pour over the meat and beans. Cover and bake for 1 hour.

6 Stir the green peppers into the stew and return to the oven for a further 15 minutes. Serve hot.

COOK'S TIP
This is the sort of stew to which you can add a variety of winter vegetables such as chunks of leek, turnip, celeriac and even little potatoes.

PROVENCAL BEEF AND OLIVE DAUBE

A daube is a French method of braising meat with wine and herbs. This version from the Nice area in the south of France also includes black olives and tomatoes.

1.5kg/3–3½lb topside beef
225g/8oz lardons, or thick streaky bacon cut into strips
225g/8oz carrots, sliced
1 bay leaf
1 thyme sprig
2 parsley stalks
3 garlic cloves
225g/8oz/2 cups pitted black olives
400g/14oz can chopped tomatoes
crusty bread, flageolet beans or pasta, to serve

FOR THE MARINADE
120ml/4fl oz/½ cup extra virgin olive oil
1 onion, sliced
4 shallots, sliced
1 celery stick, sliced
1 carrot, sliced
150ml/¼ pint/⅔ cup red wine
6 peppercorns
2 garlic cloves, sliced
1 bay leaf
1 thyme sprig
2 parsley stalks
salt

SERVES 6

1 To make the marinade, heat the oil in a large shallow pan, add the onion, shallots, celery and carrot. Cook for 2 minutes, then lower the heat and add the red wine, peppercorns, garlic, bay leaf, thyme and parsley stalks. Season with salt, then cover and leave to simmer gently for 15–20 minutes. Set aside.

3 Preheat the oven to 160°C/ 325°F/Gas 3. Lift the meat out of the marinade and fit snugly into an ovenproof casserole. Add the lardons or bacon and carrots, along with the herbs and garlic. Strain in all the marinade. Cover the casserole with greaseproof paper, then the lid and cook in the oven for 2½ hours.

2 Place the beef in a large glass or earthenware dish and pour over the cooled marinade. Cover the dish and leave to marinate in a cool place or in the fridge for 12 hours, turning the meat once or twice.

4 Remove the casserole from the oven and stir in the olives and tomatoes. Re-cover the casserole, return to the oven and cook for a further 30 minutes. Serve the meat cut into thick slices, accompanied by crusty bread, beans or pasta.

LAMB CASSEROLE WITH GARLIC AND BROAD BEANS

*This recipe has a Spanish influence and makes a substantial meal, served with potatoes. It's based on
stewing lamb with a large amount of garlic and sherry — the addition of broad beans gives colour.*

45ml/3 tbsp olive oil
1.5kg/3–3½lb fillet lamb, cut into
5cm/2in cubes
1 large onion, chopped
6 large garlic cloves, unpeeled
1 bay leaf
5ml/1 tsp paprika
120ml/4fl oz/½ cup dry sherry
115g/4oz shelled fresh or frozen
broad beans
30ml/2 tbsp chopped fresh parsley
salt and ground black pepper

SERVES 6

1   Heat 30ml/2 tbsp of the oil in a
large flameproof casserole. Add
half the meat and brown well on all
sides. Transfer to a plate. Brown the
rest of the meat in the same way and
remove from the casserole.

2   Heat the remaining oil in the
pan, add the onion and cook
for about 5 minutes until soft. Return
the meat to the casserole.

3   Add the garlic cloves, bay leaf,
paprika and sherry. Season with
salt and pepper. Bring to the boil,
then cover and simmer very gently for
1½–2 hours, until the meat is tender.

4   Add the broad beans about
10 minutes before the end of
the cooking time. Stir in the parsley
just before serving.

SPANISH PORK AND SAUSAGE CASSEROLE

Another pork dish from the Catalan region of Spain, which uses the spicy butifarra sausage. You can find these sausages in some Spanish delicatessens but, if not, sweet Italian sausages will do.

30ml/2 tbsp olive oil
4 boneless pork chops, about 175g/6oz
4 butifarra or sweet Italian sausages
1 onion, chopped
2 garlic cloves, chopped
120ml/4fl oz/½ cup dry white wine
4 plum tomatoes, chopped
1 bay leaf
30ml/2 tbsp chopped fresh parsley
salt and ground black pepper
green salad and baked potatoes,
to serve

SERVES 4

1 Heat the oil in a large deep frying pan. Cook the pork chops over a high heat until browned on both sides, then transfer to a plate.

2 Add the sausages, onion and garlic to the pan and cook over a moderate heat until the sausages are browned and the onion softened, turning the sausages two or three times during cooking. Return the chops to the pan.

3 Stir in the wine, tomatoes and bay leaf, and season with salt and pepper. Add the parsley. Cover the pan and cook for 30 minutes.

4 Remove the sausages from the pan and cut into thick slices. Return them to the pan and heat through. Serve hot, accompanied by a green salad and baked potatoes.

COOK'S TIP
Vine tomatoes, which are making a welcome appearance in our supermarkets, can be used instead of plum tomatoes.

...ITH MOZZARELLA AND TOMATO

...ls are made with beef and topped with mozzarella cheese and tomato.

1 egg, beaten
50g/2oz/⅔ cup dry breadcrumbs
vegetable oil for frying
2 beefsteak or other large
tomatoes, sliced
15ml/1 tbsp chopped fresh oregano
1 mozzarella cheese, cut into 6 slices
6 drained canned anchovies, cut in
half lengthways
salt and ground black pepper

SERVES 6

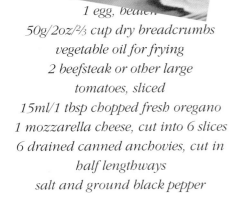

1   Preheat the oven to 200°C/
400°F/Gas 6. Put the bread and
milk into a small saucepan and heat
very gently, until the bread absorbs all
the milk. Mash it to a pulp and leave
to cool.

2   Put the beef into a bowl with
the bread mixture and the egg
and season with salt and pepper. Mix
well, then shape the mixture into six
patties. Sprinkle the breadcrumbs on
to a plate and dredge the patties,
coating them thoroughly.

3   Heat about 5mm/¼in oil in a
large frying pan. Add the patties
and fry for 2 minutes on each side,
until brown. Transfer to a greased
ovenproof dish, in a single layer.

4   Lay a slice of tomato on top of
each patty, sprinkle with
oregano and season with salt and
pepper. Place the mozzarella slices on
top. Arrange two strips of anchovy,
placed in a cross on top of each slice
of mozzarella.

5   Bake for 10–15 minutes, until
the mozzarella has melted.
Serve hot, straight from the dish.

POULTRY AND GAME

*Poultry and game play key roles in the cuisines of
all Mediterranean countries and the addition of
fruit creates sensational flavour combinations.*

Poultry and game have always played an important role in Mediterranean cooking. This is largely due to the dry, rugged and, in some places, mountainous land which does not provide good pasture. Chickens and ducks are more accessible to the poorer people of the Mediterranean who often raise them on their own land.

Chicken is without doubt the most popular type of poultry and is used creatively for Mediterranean dishes. Traditionally corn-fed, it is rich in colour and full of flavour, despite the fact that individual birds might look quite scraggy and thin. The cooking methods are varied and interesting, but they have many similarities. In both the east and west Mediterranean cooks have acknowledged the fact that chicken is perfectly complemented by the tang of fresh, dried or preserved fruits, the rich earthiness of nuts and the lively warmth of spices.

In the Middle East, chickens were kept mainly for their eggs rather than meat and generally only the older birds were cooked. This meant long, slow boiling with highly flavoured stuffings and sauces to add flavour. These recipes are now perfectly suited to improving the mild

BELOW: Verdant farmland rimmed by craggy mountains in southern Spain.

RIGHT: Lord of all he surveys, this Greek cockerel patrols his perimeter wall.

BELOW: Lemons are a favourite flavouring for chicken dishes, notably in Chicken with Lemons and Olives.

taste of our mass-produced chickens. Preserved lemons tucked in or around a whole chicken impart a fresh aromatic flavour that lacks the acidity of fresh lemons, although these can also be used successfully, adding a little sugar or honey for sweetness. Another popular flavouring for chicken is provided by the glassy, jewel-like segments of pomegranates, crushed and blended to a juice or made into a bottled preserve, having been mixed with lemon, sugar and seasoning.

From the simplest roast, served with a raisin, pine nut and sherry sauce to chorizo-flavoured casseroles, Spain has numerous excellent chicken and rabbit recipes that are popular favourites throughout the country. Duck and goose feature prominently, cooked with pears, apples or figs to counteract the richness of the meat.

Small game birds are typically Mediterranean but are used more in winter when the tourists have left. Pigeon and small game birds such as partridge and quail take their migratory route across the sea and huntsmen from all quarters of the Mediterranean take full advantage of this. Italians are particularly fond of small game and prepare some delicious pigeon dishes, lightly cooked in rich sauces and accompanied by grilled or soft polenta.

CHICKEN THIGHS WITH LEMON AND GARLIC

This recipe uses classic flavourings for chicken. Versions of it can be found in Spain and Italy.
This particular recipe, however, is of French origin.

600ml/1 pint/2½ cups chicken stock
20 large garlic cloves
25g/1oz/2 tbsp butter
15ml/1 tbsp olive oil
8 chicken thighs
1 lemon, peeled, pith removed and
sliced thinly
30ml/2 tbsp plain flour
150ml/¼ pint/⅔ cup dry white wine
salt and ground black pepper
chopped fresh parsley or basil,
to garnish
new potatoes or rice, to serve

SERVES 4

1 Put the stock into a pan and bring to the boil. Add the garlic cloves, cover and simmer gently for 40 minutes. Heat the butter and oil in a sauté or frying pan, add the chicken thighs and cook gently on all sides until golden. Transfer them to an ovenproof dish. Preheat the oven to 190°C/375°F/Gas 5.

2 Strain the stock and reserve it. Distribute the garlic and lemon slices among the chicken pieces. Add the flour to the fat in the pan in which the chicken was browned, and cook, stirring, for 1 minute. Add the wine, stirring constantly and scraping the bottom of the pan, then add the stock. Cook, stirring, until the sauce has thickened and is smooth. Season with salt and pepper.

3 Pour the sauce over the chicken, cover, and cook in the oven for 40–45 minutes. If a thicker sauce is required, lift out the chicken pieces, and reduce the sauce by boiling rapidly, until it reaches the desired consistency. Scatter over the chopped parsley or basil and serve with boiled new potatoes or rice.

OLIVE OIL ROASTED CHICKEN WITH MEDITERRANEAN VEGETABLES

*This is a delicious French alternative to a traditional roast chicken. Use a corn-fed or free-range bird,
if available. This recipe also works well with guinea fowl.*

1.75kg/4–4½lb roasting chicken
150ml/¼ pint/⅔ cup extra virgin
olive oil
½ lemon
few sprigs of fresh thyme
450g/1lb small new potatoes
1 aubergine, cut into 2.5cm/1in cubes
1 red pepper, seeded and quartered
1 fennel bulb, trimmed and quartered
8 large garlic cloves, unpeeled
coarse salt and ground black pepper

SERVES 4

2 Remove the chicken from the oven and season with salt. Turn the chicken right side up, and baste with the juices from the pan. Surround the bird with the potatoes, roll them in the pan juices, and return the roasting pan to the oven, to continue roasting.

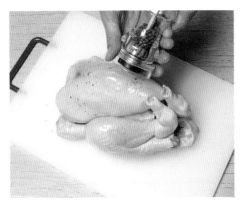

1 Preheat the oven to 200°C/ 400°F/Gas 6. Rub the chicken all over with olive oil and season with pepper. Place the lemon half inside the bird, with a sprig or two of thyme. Put the chicken breast side down in a large roasting pan. Roast for about 30 minutes.

3 After 30 minutes, add the aubergine, red pepper, fennel and garlic cloves to the pan. Drizzle with the remaining oil, and season with salt and pepper. Add any remaining thyme to the vegetables. Return to the oven, and cook for 30–50 minutes more, basting and turning the vegetables occasionally.

4 To find out if the chicken is cooked, push the tip of a sharp knife between the thigh and breast. If the juices run clear, it is done. The vegetables should be tender and just beginning to brown. Serve the chicken and vegetables from the pan, or transfer the vegetables to a serving dish, joint the chicken and place it on top. Serve the skimmed juices in a gravy boat.

CHICKEN WITH CHORIZO

The addition of chorizo sausage and sherry gives a warm, interesting flavour to this simple Spanish casserole. Serve with rice or boiled potatoes.

1 medium chicken, jointed, or
4 chicken legs, halved
10ml/2 tsp ground paprika
60ml/4 tbsp olive oil
2 small onions, sliced
6 garlic cloves, thinly sliced
150g/5oz chorizo sausage
400g/14oz can chopped tomatoes
12–16 bay leaves
75ml/5 tbsp medium sherry
salt and ground black pepper
rice or potatoes, to serve

SERVES 4

1 Preheat the oven to 190°C/ 375°F/Gas 5. Coat the chicken pieces in the paprika, making sure they are evenly covered, then season with salt. Heat the olive oil in a frying pan and fry the chicken until brown.

2 Transfer to an ovenproof dish. Add the onions to the pan and fry quickly. Add the garlic and sliced chorizo and fry for 2 minutes.

3 Add the tomatoes, two of the bay leaves and sherry and bring to the boil. Pour over the chicken and cover with a lid. Bake for 45 minutes. Remove the lid and season to taste. Cook for a further 20 minutes until the chicken is tender and golden. Serve with rice or potatoes, garnished with bay leaves.

CHICKEN CASSEROLE WITH SPICED FIGS

The Spanish Catalans have various recipes for fruit with meat. This is quite an unusual one, but it uses one of the fruits most strongly associated with the Mediterranean — the fig.

FOR THE FIGS
150g/5oz/²⁄₃ cup granulated sugar
120ml/4fl oz/½ cup white
wine vinegar
1 lemon slice
1 cinnamon stick
450g/1lb fresh figs

FOR THE CHICKEN
120ml/4fl oz/½ cup medium sweet
white wine
pared rind of ½ lemon
1.5kg/3–3½lb chicken, jointed into
eight pieces
50g/2oz lardons, or thick streaky
bacon cut into strips
15ml/1 tbsp olive oil
50ml/2fl oz/¼ cup chicken stock
salt and ground black pepper

SERVES 4

1 Put the sugar, vinegar, lemon slice and cinnamon stick in a pan with 120ml/4fl oz/½ cup water. Bring to the boil, then simmer for 5 minutes. Add the figs, cover, and simmer for 10 minutes. Remove from heat, cover, and leave for 3 hours.

2 Preheat the oven to 180°C/ 350°F/Gas 4. Drain the figs, and place in a bowl. Add the wine and lemon rind. Season the chicken. In a large frying pan cook the lardons or streaky bacon strips until the fat melts and they turn golden. Transfer to a shallow ovenproof dish, leaving any fat in the pan. Add the oil to the pan and brown the chicken pieces all over.

3 Drain the figs, adding the wine to the pan with the chicken. Boil until the sauce has reduced and is syrupy. Transfer the contents of the frying pan to the ovenproof dish and cook in the oven, uncovered, for about 20 minutes. Add the figs and chicken stock, cover and return to the oven for a further 10 minutes. Serve with a green salad.

CHICKEN AND APRICOT FILO PIE

The filling for this pie has a Middle Eastern flavour — minced chicken combined with apricots, bulgur wheat, nuts and spices.

75g/3oz/½ cup bulgur wheat
75g/3oz/6 tbsp butter
1 onion, chopped
450g/1lb minced chicken
50g/2oz/¼ cup ready-to-eat dried apricots, finely chopped
25g/1oz/¼ cup blanched almonds, chopped
5ml/1 tsp ground cinnamon
2.5ml/½ tsp ground allspice
50ml/2fl oz/¼ cup Greek yogurt
15ml/1 tbsp snipped fresh chives
30ml/2 tbsp chopped fresh parsley
6 large sheets filo pastry
salt and ground black pepper
chives, to garnish

SERVES 6

1 Preheat the oven to 200°C/400°F/Gas 6. Put the bulgur wheat in a bowl with 120ml/4fl oz/½ cup boiling water. Soak for 5–10 minutes, until the water is absorbed.

2 Heat 25g/1oz/2 tbsp of the butter in a pan, and gently fry the onion and chicken until pale golden.

3 Stir in the apricots, almonds and bulgur wheat and cook for a further 2 minutes. Remove from the heat and stir in the cinnamon, allspice, yogurt, chives and parsley. Season to taste with salt and pepper.

4 Melt the remaining butter. Unroll the filo pastry and cut into 25cm/10in rounds. Keep the pastry rounds covered with a clean, damp dish towel to prevent drying.

5 Line a 23cm/9in loose-based flan tin with three of the pastry rounds, brushing each one with butter as you layer them. Spoon in the chicken mixture, cover with three more pastry rounds, brushed with melted butter as before.

6 Crumple the remaining rounds and place them on top of the pie, then brush over any remaining melted butter. Bake the pie for about 30 minutes, until the pastry is golden brown and crisp. Serve Chicken and Apricot Filo Pie hot or cold, cut in wedges and garnished with chives.

CIRCASSIAN CHICKEN

This is a Turkish dish, which is popular all over the Middle East. The chicken is poached and served cold with a flavoursome walnut sauce.

1.5kg/3–3½ lb chicken
2 onions, quartered
1 carrot, sliced
1 celery stick, trimmed and sliced
6 peppercorns
3 slices bread, crusts removed
2 garlic cloves, roughly chopped
400g/14oz/3½ cups chopped walnuts
15ml/1 tbsp walnut oil
salt and ground black pepper
chopped walnuts and paprika,
to garnish

SERVES 6

1 Place the chicken in a large pan, with the onions, carrot, celery and peppercorns. Add enough water to cover, and bring to the boil. Simmer for about 1 hour, uncovered, until the chicken is tender. Leave to cool in the stock. Drain the chicken, reserving the stock.

2 Tear up the bread and soak in 90ml/6 tbsp of the chicken stock. Transfer to a blender or food processor, with the garlic and walnuts, and add 250ml/8fl oz/1 cup of the remaining stock. Process until smooth, then transfer to a pan.

3 Over a low heat, gradually add more chicken stock to the sauce, stirring constantly, until it is of a thick pouring consistency. Season with salt and pepper, remove from the heat and leave to cool in the pan. Skin and bone the chicken, and cut into bite-size chunks.

4 Place in a bowl and add a little of the sauce. Stir to coat the chicken, then arrange on a serving dish. Spoon the remaining sauce over the chicken, and drizzle with the walnut oil. Sprinkle with walnuts and paprika and serve at once.

CHICKEN WITH LEMONS AND OLIVES

Preserved lemons and limes are frequently used in Mediterranean cookery, particularly in North Africa where their gentle flavour enhances all kinds of meat and fish dishes.

2.5ml/½ tsp ground cinnamon
2.5ml/½ tsp ground turmeric
1.5kg/3–3½lb chicken
30ml/2 tbsp olive oil
1 large onion, thinly sliced
5cm/2in piece fresh root
ginger, grated
600ml/1 pint/2½ cups chicken stock
2 preserved lemons or limes, or fresh,
cut into wedges
75g/3oz/½ cup pitted brown olives
15ml/1 tbsp clear honey
60ml/4 tbsp chopped fresh coriander
salt and ground black pepper
coriander sprigs, to garnish

SERVES 4

1 Preheat the oven to 190°C/ 375°F/Gas 5. Mix the ground cinnamon and turmeric in a bowl with a little salt and pepper and rub all over the chicken skin to give an even coating.

2 Heat the oil in a large sauté or shallow frying pan and fry the chicken on all sides until it turns golden. Transfer the chicken to an ovenproof dish.

3 Add the sliced onion to the pan and fry for 3 minutes. Stir in the grated ginger and the chicken stock and bring just to the boil. Pour over the chicken, cover with a lid and bake in the oven for 30 minutes.

4 Remove the chicken from the oven and add the lemons or limes, brown olives and honey. Bake, uncovered, for a further 45 minutes until the chicken is tender.

5 Stir in the coriander and season to taste. Garnish with coriander sprigs and serve at once.

CASSOULET

Cassoulet is a classic French dish in which a feast of various meats is baked slowly with beans under a golden crumb crust. It is hearty and rich, perfect for a winter gathering.

675g/1½lb/3½ cups dried
haricot beans
900g/2lb salt belly pork
4 large duck breasts
60ml/4 tbsp olive oil
2 onions, chopped
6 garlic cloves, crushed
2 bay leaves
1.5ml/¼ tsp ground cloves
60ml/4 tbsp tomato purée
8 good-quality sausages
4 tomatoes
75g/3oz/1½ cups stale breadcrumbs
salt and ground black pepper

SERVES 6–8

1 Put the beans in a large bowl and cover with plenty of cold water. Leave to soak overnight. If using salted belly pork, soak it overnight in water.

2 Drain the beans thoroughly and put them in a large saucepan with fresh water to cover. Bring to the boil and boil rapidly for 10 minutes. Drain and set the beans aside.

3 Cut the pork into large pieces, discarding the rind. Halve the duck breasts.

4 Heat 30ml/2 tbsp of the oil in a frying pan and fry the pork in batches, until browned.

5 Put the beans in a large, heavy-based saucepan with the onions, garlic, bay leaves, ground cloves and tomato purée. Stir in the browned pork and just cover with water. Bring to the boil, then reduce the heat to the lowest setting and simmer, covered, for about 1½ hours until the beans are tender.

6 Preheat the oven to 180°C/350°F/Gas 4. Heat the rest of the oil in a frying pan and fry the duck breasts and sausages until browned. Cut the sausages into smaller pieces.

7 Plunge the tomatoes into boiling water for 30 seconds, then refresh in cold water. Peel away the skins and cut them into quarters.

8 Transfer the bean mixture to a large earthenware pot or ovenproof dish and stir in the fried sausages and duck breasts and chopped tomatoes with salt and pepper to taste.

9 Sprinkle with an even layer of breadcrumbs and bake in the oven for 45 minutes to 1 hour until the crust is golden. Serve hot.

VARIATION
You can easily alter the proportions and types of meat and vegetables in a cassoulet. Turnips, carrots and celeriac make suitable vegetable substitutes while cubed lamb and goose can replace the pork and duck.

CHICKEN IN A SALT CRUST

Cooking food in a casing of salt gives a deliciously moist, tender flavour that, surprisingly, is not too salty. The technique is used in both Italy and France for chicken and whole fish, although chicken is easier to deal with.

1.75kg/4–4½lb chicken
about 2.25kg/5lb coarse sea salt

FOR THE GARLIC PUREE
450g/1lb onions, quartered
2 large heads of garlic
120ml/4fl oz/½ cup olive oil
salt and ground black pepper

FOR THE ROASTED TOMATOES
AND PEPPERS
450g/1lb plum tomatoes
3 red peppers, seeded and quartered
1 red chilli, seeded and finely chopped
90ml/6 tbsp olive oil
flat leaf parsley, to garnish

SERVES 6

 2 Truss the chicken tightly so that the salt cannot fall into the cavity. Sprinkle a thin layer of salt in the foil-lined dish then place the chicken on top.

3 Pour the remaining salt all around and over the top of the chicken until it is completely encased. Sprinkle the top with a little water.

4 Cover tightly with the foil and bake the chicken on the lower oven shelf for 1¾ hours. Meanwhile, put the onions in a small heavy-based saucepan. Break up the heads of garlic, but leave the skins on. Add to the pan with the olive oil and a little salt and pepper.

5 Cover and cook over the lowest possible heat for about 1 hour or until the garlic is completely soft.

1 Preheat the oven to 220°C/ 425°F/Gas 7. Choose a deep ovenproof dish into which the whole chicken will fit snugly. Line the dish with a double thickness of heavy foil, allowing plenty of excess foil to overhang the top edge of the ovenproof dish.

COOK'S TIP
This recipe makes a really stunning main course when you want to serve something a little different. Take the salt-crusted chicken to the table garnished with plenty of fresh mixed herbs. Once you've scraped away the salt, transfer the chicken to a clean plate to carve it.

 6 Plunge the tomatoes into boiling water for 30 seconds, then refresh in cold water. Peel away the skins and quarter. Put the red peppers, tomatoes and chilli in a shallow ovenproof dish and sprinkle with the oil. Bake on the shelf above the chicken for 45 minutes or until the peppers are slightly charred.

7 Squeeze the garlic out of the skins. Process the onions, garlic and pan juices in a blender or food processor until smooth. Return the purée to the clean saucepan.

8 To serve the chicken, open out the foil and ease it out of the dish. Place on a large serving platter. Transfer the roasted pepper mixture to a serving dish and garnish with parsley. Reheat the garlic purée. Crack open the salt crust on the chicken and brush away the salt before carving and serving with the garlic purée and pepper mixture.

SPICED DUCK WITH PEARS

This delicious casserole is based on a Catalan dish that uses goose or duck. The sautéed pears are added towards the end of cooking, along with picarda sauce, a pounded pine nut and garlic paste which both flavours and thickens.

6 duck portions, either breast or
leg pieces
15ml/1 tbsp olive oil
1 large onion, thinly sliced
1 cinnamon stick, halved
2 thyme sprigs
475ml/16fl oz/2 cups chicken stock

TO FINISH
3 firm ripe pears
30ml/2 tbsp olive oil
2 garlic cloves, sliced
25g/1oz/⅓ cup pine nuts
2.5ml/½ tsp saffron strands
25g/1oz/2 tbsp raisins
salt and ground black pepper
young thyme sprigs or parsley,
to garnish

SERVES 6

1 Preheat the oven to 180°C/ 350°F/Gas 4. Fry the duck portions in the olive oil for about 5 minutes until the skin is golden. Transfer the duck to an ovenproof dish and drain off all but 15ml/1 tbsp of the fat left in the pan.

2 Add the onion to the pan and fry for 5 minutes. Add the cinnamon stick, thyme and stock and bring to the boil. Pour over the duck and bake in the oven for 1¼ hours.

3 Meanwhile, peel, core and halve the pears and fry quickly in the oil until beginning to turn golden on the cut sides. Pound the garlic, pine nuts and saffron in a mortar, with a pestle, to make a thick, smooth paste.

4 Add the paste to the casserole along with the raisins and pears. Bake for a further 15 minutes until the pears are tender.

5 Season to taste with salt and pepper and garnish with parsley or thyme. Serve with mashed potatoes and a green vegetable, if liked.

COOK'S TIP
A good stock is essential for this dish. Buy a large duck (plus two extra duck breasts if you want portions to be generous) and joint it yourself, using the giblets and carcass for stock. Alternatively buy duck portions and a carton of chicken stock.

RABBIT SALMOREJO

Small pieces of jointed rabbit, conveniently sold in packs at the supermarket, make an interesting alternative to chicken in this light, spicy sauté from Spain. Serve with a simple dressed salad.

675g/1½lb rabbit portions
300ml/½ pint/1¼ cups dry white wine
15ml/1 tbsp sherry vinegar
several oregano sprigs
2 bay leaves
90ml/6 tbsp olive oil
175g/6oz baby onions, peeled and left whole
1 red chilli, seeded and finely chopped
4 garlic cloves, sliced
10ml/2 tsp paprika
150ml/¼ pint/⅔ cup chicken stock
salt and ground black pepper
flat leaf parsley sprigs, to garnish

SERVES 4

1 Put the rabbit in a bowl. Add the wine, vinegar, oregano and bay leaves and toss together lightly. Cover and leave to marinate for several hours or overnight.

2 Drain the rabbit, reserving the marinade, and pat dry on kitchen paper. Heat the oil in a large sauté or frying pan. Add the rabbit and fry on all sides until golden, then remove with a slotted spoon. Fry the onions until beginning to colour.

3 Remove the onions from the pan and add the chilli, garlic and paprika. Cook, stirring for about a minute. Add the reserved marinade, with the stock. Season lightly.

4 Return the rabbit to the pan with the onions. Bring to the boil, then reduce the heat and cover with a lid. Simmer very gently for about 45 minutes until the rabbit is tender. Serve garnished with a few sprigs of flat leaf parsley, if you like.

COOK'S TIP
If more convenient, rather than cooking on the hob, transfer the stew to an ovenproof dish and bake in the oven at 180°C/350°F/Gas 4 for about 50 minutes.

DUCK BREASTS WITH A WALNUT AND POMEGRANATE SAUCE

This is an extremely exotic sweet and sour dish which originally came from Persia.

60ml/4 tbsp olive oil
2 onions, very thinly sliced
2.5ml/½ tsp ground turmeric
400g/14oz/3½ cups walnuts, roughly chopped
1 litre/1¾ pints/4 cups duck or chicken stock
6 pomegranates
30ml/2 tbsp caster sugar
60ml/4 tbsp lemon juice
4 duck breasts, about 225g/8oz each
salt and ground black pepper

COOK'S TIP
Choose pomegranates with shiny, brightly coloured skins. The juice stains, so take care when cutting them. Only the seeds are used in cooking, the pith is discarded.

1 Heat half the oil in a frying pan. Add the onions and turmeric, and cook gently until soft. Transfer to a pan, add the walnuts and stock, then season with salt and pepper. Stir, then bring to the boil and simmer the mixture, uncovered, for 20 minutes.

2 Cut the pomegranates in half and scoop out the seeds into a bowl. Reserve the seeds of one pomegranate. Transfer the remaining seeds to a blender or food processor, and process to break them up. Strain through a sieve, to extract the juice, and stir in the sugar and lemon juice.

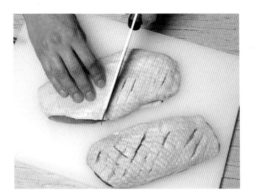

3 Score the skin of the duck breasts in a lattice fashion with a sharp knife. Heat the remaining oil in a frying pan or char grill and place the duck breasts in it, skin side down.

4 Cook gently for 10 minutes, pouring off the fat from time to time, until the skin is dark golden and crisp. Turn them over and cook for a further 3–4 minutes. Transfer to a plate and leave to rest.

5 Deglaze the frying pan or char grill with the pomegranate juice mixture, stirring with a wooden spoon, then add the walnut and stock mixture and simmer for 15 minutes until the sauce has thickened slightly. Serve the duck breasts sliced, drizzled with a little sauce, and garnished with the reserved pomegranate seeds. Serve the remaining sauce separately.

PIGEON BREASTS WITH PANCETTA

Mild succulent pigeon breasts are easy to cook and make an impressive main course for a special dinner.
Serve this Italian-style dish with polenta and some simple green vegetables.

4 whole pigeons
2 large onions
2 carrots, roughly chopped
1 celery stick, trimmed and
roughly chopped
25g/1oz dried porcini mushrooms
50g/2oz pancetta
25g/1oz/2 tbsp butter
30ml/2 tbsp olive oil
2 garlic cloves, crushed
150ml/¼ pint/⅔ cup red wine
salt and ground black pepper
flat leaf parsley, to garnish
cooked oyster mushrooms, to serve

SERVES 4

1. To prepare a pigeon, cut down the length of the bird, just to one side of the breastbone. Gradually scrape away the meat from the breastbone until the breast comes away completely. Do the same on the other side then repeat with the remaining pigeons.

2. Put the pigeon carcasses in a large saucepan. Halve one of the onions, leaving the skin on. Add to the pan with the carrots and celery and just cover with water. Bring to the boil, reduce the heat and simmer very gently, uncovered, for about 1½ hours to make a dark, rich stock. Leave to cool slightly, then strain through a large sieve into a bowl.

3. Cover the dried mushrooms with 150ml/¼ pint/⅔ cup hot water and soak for 30 minutes. Cut the pancetta into small dice.

4. Peel and finely chop the remaining onion. Melt half the butter with the oil in a large frying pan. Add the onion and pancetta and fry very gently for 3 minutes. Add the pigeon breasts, skin sides down and fry for 2 minutes until browned. Turn over and fry for a further 2 minutes.

5. Add the mushrooms, with the soaking liquid, garlic, wine and 250ml/8fl oz/1 cup of the stock. Bring just to the boil, then reduce the heat and simmer gently for 5 minutes until the pigeon breasts are tender, but still a little pink in the centre.

6. Lift out the pigeon breasts and keep them hot. Return the sauce to the boil and boil rapidly to reduce slightly. Gradually whisk in all the remaining butter and season with salt and pepper to taste.

7. Transfer the pigeon breasts to warmed serving plates and pour over the sauce. Serve at once, garnished with sprigs of parsley and accompanied by oyster mushrooms.

COOK'S TIP
If buying pigeons from a butcher, order them in advance and ask him to remove the breasts for you. You can also joint the legs and fry these with the breasts, although there is little meat on them and you might prefer to let them flavour the stock.

MOROCCAN PIGEON PIE

This recipe is based upon a classic Moroccan dish called Pastilla, which is a filo pastry pie, filled with an unusual but delicious mixture of pigeon, eggs, spices and nuts. If pigeon is unavailable, chicken makes a good substitute.

3 pigeons
50g/2oz/4 tbsp butter
1 onion, chopped
1 cinnamon stick
2.5ml/½ tsp ground ginger
30ml/2 tbsp chopped fresh coriander
45ml/3 tbsp chopped fresh parsley
pinch of ground turmeric
15ml/1 tbsp caster sugar
1.5ml/¼ tsp ground cinnamon
115g/4oz/1 cup toasted almonds,
finely chopped
6 eggs, beaten
salt and ground black pepper
cinnamon and icing sugar, to garnish

FOR THE PASTRY
175g/6oz/¾ cup butter, melted
16 sheets filo pastry
1 egg yolk

SERVES 6

1 Wash the pigeons and place in a pan with the butter, onion, cinnamon stick, ginger, coriander, parsley and turmeric. Season with salt and pepper. Add just enough water to cover and bring to the boil. Cover and simmer gently for about 1 hour, until the pigeon flesh is very tender.

2 Strain off the stock and reserve. Skin and bone the pigeons, and shred the flesh into bite-size pieces. Preheat the oven to 180°C/350°F/ Gas 4. Mix together the sugar, cinnamon and almonds, and set aside.

3 Measure 150ml/¼ pint/⅔ cup of the reserved stock into a small pan. Add the eggs and mix well. Stir over a low heat until creamy and very thick and almost set. Season with salt and pepper.

4 Brush a 30cm/12in diameter ovenproof dish with some of the melted butter and lay the first sheet of pastry in the dish. Brush this with butter and continue with five more sheets of pastry. Cover with the almond mixture, then half the egg mixture. Moisten with a little stock.

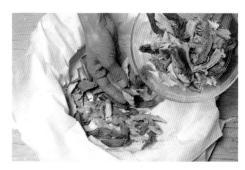

5 Layer four more sheets of filo pastry, brushing with butter as before. Lay the pigeon meat on top, then add the remaining egg mixture and more stock. Cover with all the remaining pastry, brushing each sheet with butter, and tuck in any overlap.

6 Brush the pie with egg yolk and bake for 40 minutes. Raise the oven temperature to 200°C/400°F/ Gas 6, and bake for 15 minutes more, until the pastry is crisp and golden. Garnish with a lattice design of cinnamon and icing sugar. Serve hot.

GRAINS AND PULSES

*Mediterranean countries deserve thanks for the
creation of risotto, paella, pizzas and pasta, and
the many salads and stews based on dried pulses.*

The countries surrounding the Mediterranean produce a seemingly inexhaustible quantity and variety of grains and pulses. Wheat, the most ancient cereal grown in the region, predominates. It is the staple that provides for traditional and specialised local dishes, but from centuries of trading and travel come a great number of dishes which, although originally associated with one country, are often made using slightly different techniques and ingredients in many different areas of the Mediterranean.

Pasta, for example, although most widely consumed in Italy, is also made in the eastern Mediterranean under the name of *rishta*; it is known in Spain as *fideos*, and in Egypt as *macaroni* or *koshari*.

Bread is a staple food all over the Mediterranean. When you consider that it is made using the same basic ingredients, it is remarkable that there is such a variety of flavours and textures. There are the Italian olive breads – focaccia and ciabatta – and the dry breads like grissini and crostini, as well as a feast of soft breads, richly flavoured with sun-dried tomatoes and herbs. Visit any

BELOW: Spain produces a wide range of grains of all types, seen here at a typical market.

part of France and see how important freshly baked breads, from rich brioches to crisp baguettes, are to the French. Bakeries stay open all through the day, turning out batch after batch of hot loaves. French bakers do not depend on preservatives so bread has to be prepared fresh for every meal. Festive breads are still widely enjoyed. The most elaborate is the braided Greek Easter Bread, flavoured with nuts and fruit and adorned with hard-boiled eggs that are dyed red. According to legend, these will keep those who eat them safe from harm.

The unleavened or slightly leavened flat breads of the eastern Mediterranean and North Africa are eaten with every meal. The most common of these is the pitta which varies in shape and size. The Turks bake a huge, flat loaf that inflates like a balloon during baking: this is carried ceremoniously to the table where it is shared by the diners; its soft, chewy dough is perfect for mopping up spicy sauces. Pitta bread is often used instead of knives and forks; when slit, the empty pocket makes a perfect container for salads, bean dishes, falafel and meats.

Wheat flour is also used to make the highly popular filo pastries of North Africa, Lebanon, Greece and Turkey. It is skilfully shaped and stretched to form a transparent sheet which is then brushed with olive oil or melted butter and folded into layers. When cooked, it resembles puff pastry, light and crisp. Filo is used in many sweet or savoury classics like the Moroccan Pastilla, a spicy pigeon pie with cloves and cinnamon.

Regional classics like North African Couscous are also made with wheat. Couscous is a kind of coarsely ground wheat that gives its name to the traditional dish of either a spiced meat or vegetable sauce that covers the steamed grain. At its most splendid it is served as a finale to a special feast when guests have already enjoyed several delicate courses. The couscous is piled high on a large platter and topped with meat or vegetables smothered with a delectable sweet, spicy sauce.

ABOVE: The fertile Guadalquivir valley in Spain.

Rice has been central to Mediterranean cookery for as long as twelve thousand years. The Moors brought rice to Europe in the eighth century through the eastern Mediterranean from Persia and Asia. With its strong Moorish tradition, southern Spain, particularly Valencia, remains the country's main producer of rice. The national dish of Paella originates from the coastal cities and fishing ports of Andalucia. But the uses for rice extend much further than one national dish. Many other rich, saffron-flavoured risottos are widely popular, and are good with Zarzuela, an extravagant feast of fish and crustacea. Italians also consume a lot of rice, predominantly arborio, a short grain, starchy rice that cooks down to a soft creamy consistency. Arborio supplies the authentic taste of the classic subtle accompaniment Risotto alla Milanese, which is enriched with saffron, wine and Parmesan. In contrast, the fiery, dry pilaffs of Turkey and the Middle East are heavily spiced and mixed with numerous herbs, dried fruits, nuts and vegetables.

Chick-peas are perhaps the most popular of the Mediterranean pulses and form the basis of creamy pastes like Hummus. Along with other pulses and beans they are widely used in cold, garlicky dressed salads and as the base of many soups.

Traditionally a peasant food, beans are given long slow cooking and their taste is enhanced with cheap but flavoursome meats or garlic-cured sausages. Served with locally produced vegetables, beans are the heart of many delicious soups and stews; for example, the traditional Cassoulet of France.

Before cooking dried beans, soak them in water overnight. Boil them rapidly for ten minutes to drive off any toxins, then reduce the heat and simmer for the rest of the recommended cooking time. Only add salt towards the end of the cooking time – if added too soon salt will toughen the beans.

HUMMUS BI TAHINA

Blending chick-peas with garlic and oil makes a surprisingly creamy purée that is delicious as part of a Turkish-style mezze, or as a dip with vegetables. Leftovers make a good sandwich filler.

150g/5oz/¾ cup dried chick-peas
juice of 2 lemons
2 garlic cloves, sliced
30ml/2 tbsp olive oil
pinch of cayenne pepper
150ml/¼ pint/⅔ cup tahini paste
salt and ground black pepper
extra olive oil and cayenne pepper
for sprinkling
flat leaf parsley, to garnish

SERVES 4–6

1 Put the chick-peas in a bowl with plenty of cold water and leave to soak overnight.

2 Drain the chick-peas and cover with fresh water in a saucepan. Bring to the boil and boil rapidly for 10 minutes. Reduce the heat and simmer gently for about 1 hour until soft. Drain.

3 Process the chick-peas in a food processor to a smooth purée. Add the lemon juice, garlic, olive oil, cayenne pepper and tahini and blend until creamy, scraping the mixture down from the sides of the bowl.

4 Season the purée with salt and pepper and transfer to a serving dish. Sprinkle with oil and cayenne pepper and serve garnished with a few parsley sprigs.

COOK'S TIP
For convenience, canned chick-peas can be used instead. Allow two 400g/14oz cans and drain them thoroughly. Tahini paste can now be purchased from most supermarkets or health food shops.

FALAFEL

*In North Africa these spicy fritters are made using dried broad beans, but chick-peas are much easier
to buy. They are lovely served as a snack with garlicky yogurt or stuffed into warmed pitta bread.*

150g/5oz/¾ cup dried chick-peas
1 large onion, roughly chopped
2 garlic cloves, roughly chopped
60ml/4 tbsp roughly chopped parsley
5ml/1 tsp cumin seeds, crushed
5ml/1 tsp coriander seeds, crushed
2.5ml/½ tsp baking powder
salt and ground black pepper
oil for deep frying
pitta bread, salad and yogurt, to serve

SERVES 4

1 Put the chick-peas in a bowl with plenty of cold water. Leave to soak overnight.

2 Drain the chick-peas and cover with water in a pan. Bring to the boil. Boil rapidly for 10 minutes. Reduce the heat and simmer for about 1 hour until soft. Drain.

3 Place in a food processor with the onion, garlic, parsley, cumin, coriander and baking powder. Add salt and pepper to taste. Process until the mixture forms a firm paste.

4 Shape the mixture into walnut-size balls and flatten them slightly. In a deep pan, heat 5cm/2in oil until a little of the mixture sizzles on the surface. Fry the falafel in batches until golden. Drain on kitchen paper and keep hot while frying the remainder. Serve warm in pitta bread, with salad and yogurt.

SUN-DRIED TOMATO BREAD

In the south of Italy, tomatoes are often dried off in the hot sun. They are then preserved in oil, or hung up in strings in the kitchen, to use in the winter. This recipe uses the former.

675g/1½lb/6 cups strong plain flour
10ml/2 tsp salt
25g/1oz/2 tbsp caster sugar
25g/1oz fresh yeast
400–475ml/14–16fl oz/1⅔–2 cups warm milk
15ml/1 tbsp tomato purée
75ml/5 tbsp oil from the jar of sun-dried tomatoes
75ml/5 tbsp extra virgin olive oil
75g/3oz/¾ cup drained sun-dried tomatoes, chopped
1 large onion, chopped

MAKES 4 SMALL LOAVES

 Sift the flour, salt and sugar into a bowl, and make a well in the centre. Crumble the yeast, mix with 150ml/¼ pint/⅔ cup of the warm milk and add to the flour.

COOK'S TIP
Use a pair of sharp kitchen scissors to cut up the sun-dried tomatoes.

2 Mix the tomato purée into the remaining milk, until evenly blended, then add to the flour with the tomato oil and olive oil.

3 Gradually mix the flour into the liquid ingredients, until you have a dough. Turn out on to a floured surface, and knead for about 10 minutes, until smooth and elastic. Return to the clean bowl, cover with a cloth, and leave to rise in a warm place for about 2 hours.

4 Knock the dough back, and add the tomatoes and onion. Knead until evenly distributed through the dough. Shape into four rounds and place on a greased baking sheet. Cover with a dish towel and leave to rise again for about 45 minutes.

5 Preheat the oven to 190°C/375°F/Gas 5. Bake the bread for 45 minutes, or until the loaves sound hollow when you tap them underneath with your fingers. Leave to cool on a wire rack. Eat warm, or toasted with grated mozzarella cheese on top.

GREEK EASTER BREAD

In Greece, Easter celebrations are very important, and involve much preparation in the kitchen. This bread is sold in all the bakers' shops, and also made at home. It is traditionally decorated with red dyed eggs.

25g/1oz fresh yeast
120ml/4fl oz/½ cup warm milk
675g/1½lb /6 cups strong plain flour
2 eggs, beaten
2.5ml/½ tsp caraway seeds
15ml/1 tbsp caster sugar
15ml/1 tbsp brandy
50g/2oz/4 tbsp butter, melted
1 egg white, beaten
2–3 hard-boiled eggs, dyed red
50g/2oz/½ cup split almonds

MAKES 1 LOAF

 Crumble the yeast into a bowl. Mix with one or two tablespoons of warm water, until softened. Add the milk and 115g/4oz/1 cup of the flour and mix to a creamy consistency. Cover with a cloth, and leave in a warm place to rise for 1 hour.

COOK'S TIP
You can often buy fresh yeast from bakers' shops. It should be pale cream in colour with a firm but crumbly texture.

2 Sift the remaining flour into a large bowl and make a well in the centre. Pour the risen yeast into the well, and draw in a little of the flour from the sides. Add the eggs, caraway seeds, sugar, and brandy. Incorporate the remaining flour, until the mixture begins to form a dough.

3 Mix in the melted butter. Turn on to a floured surface, and knead for about 10 minutes, until the dough becomes smooth. Return to the bowl, and cover with a cloth. Leave in a warm place for 3 hours.

4 Preheat the oven to 180°C/ 350°F/Gas 4. Knock back the dough, turn on to a floured surface and knead for a minute or two. Divide the dough into three, and roll each piece into a long sausage. Make a plait as shown above, and place the loaf on a greased baking sheet.

5 Tuck the ends under, brush with the egg white and decorate with the eggs and split almonds. Bake for about 1 hour, until the loaf sounds hollow when tapped on the bottom. Cool on a wire rack.

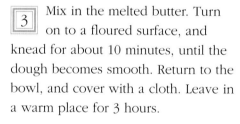

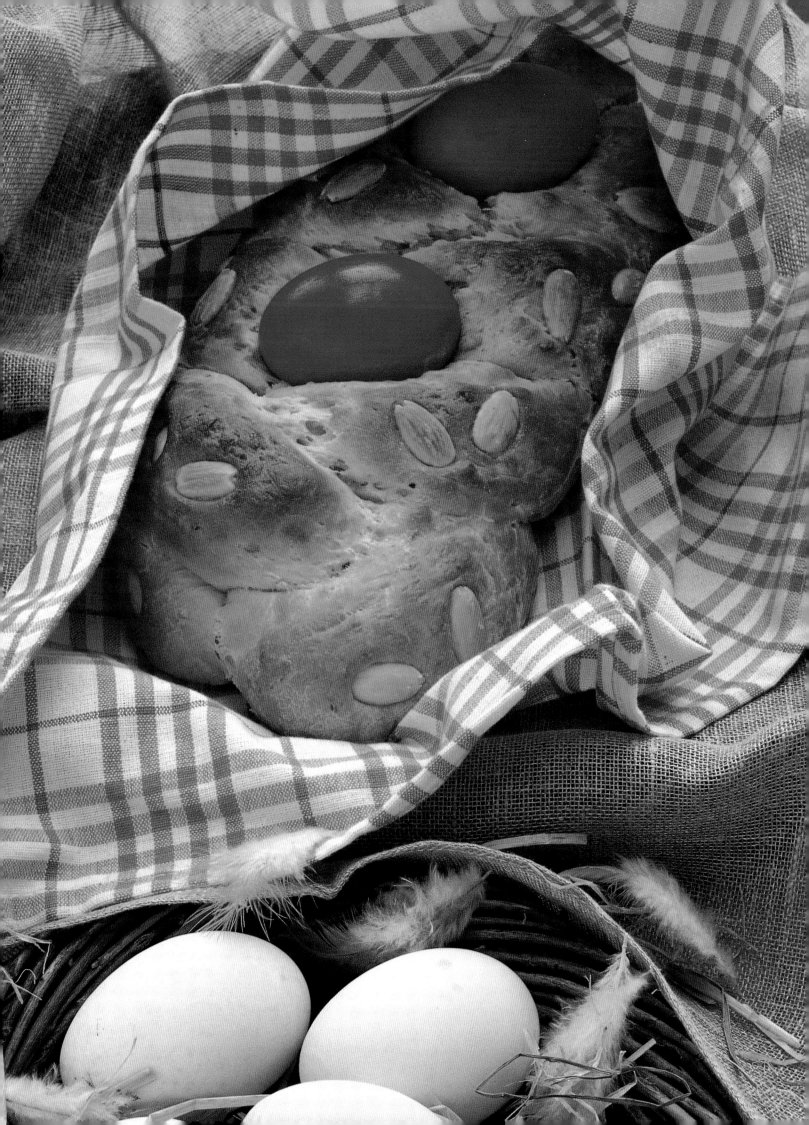

FOCACCIA

—

This is a flattish bread, originating from Genoa in Italy, made with flour, olive oil and salt. There
are many variations, from many regions, including stuffed varieties, and versions topped with onions,
olives or herbs.

25g/1oz fresh yeast
400g/14oz/3½ cups strong plain flour
10ml/2 tsp salt
75ml/5 tbsp olive oil
10ml/2 tsp coarse sea salt

MAKES 1 ROUND 25CM/10IN LOAF

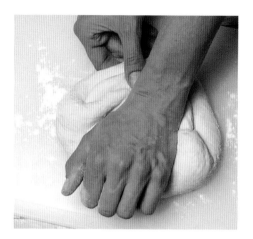

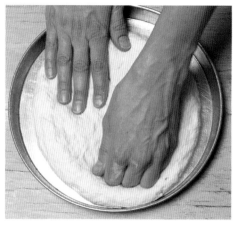

1 Dissolve the yeast in 120ml/
4fl oz/½ cup warm water. Allow
to stand for 10 minutes. Sift the flour
into a large bowl, make a well in the
centre, and add the yeast, salt and
30ml/2 tbsp oil. Mix in the flour and
add more water to make a dough.

2 Turn out on to a floured surface
and knead the dough for about
10 minutes, until smooth and elastic.
Return to the bowl, cover with a
cloth, and leave to rise in a warm
place for 2–2½ hours until the dough
has doubled in bulk.

3 Knock back the dough and
knead again for a few minutes.
Press into an oiled 25cm/10in tart tin,
and cover with a damp cloth. Leave
to rise for 30 minutes.

4 Preheat the oven to 200°C/
400°F/Gas 6. Poke the dough
all over with your fingers, to make
little dimples in the surface. Pour the
remaining oil over the dough, using a
pastry brush to take it to the edges.
Sprinkle with the salt.

5 Bake for 20–25 minutes, until
the bread is a pale gold.
Carefully remove from the tin and
leave to cool on a rack. The bread is
best eaten on the same day, but it
also freezes very well.

ONION FOCACCIA

This pizza-like flat bread is characterized by its soft dimpled surface, sometimes dredged simply with coarse salt, or with onions, herbs or olives. It tastes delicious served warm with soups and stews.

675g/1½lb/6 cups strong plain flour
2.5ml/½ tsp salt
2.5ml/½ tsp caster sugar
15ml/1 tbsp easy-blend dried yeast
60ml/4 tbsp extra virgin olive oil
450ml/¾ pint/1⅞ cups hand-
hot water

TO FINISH
2 red onions, thinly sliced
45ml/3 tbsp extra virgin olive oil
15ml/1 tbsp coarse salt

MAKES TWO 25CM/10IN LOAVES

1 Sift the flour, salt and sugar into a large bowl. Stir in the yeast, oil and water and mix to a dough using a round-bladed knife. (Add a little extra water if the dough is dry.)

2 Turn out on to a lightly floured surface and knead for about 10 minutes until smooth and elastic.

3 Put the dough in a clean, lightly oiled bowl and cover with clear film. Leave to rise in a warm place until doubled in bulk.

4 Place two 25cm/10in plain metal flan rings on baking sheets. Oil the insides of the rings and the baking sheets.

5 Preheat the oven to 200°C/ 400°F/Gas 6. Halve the dough and roll each piece to a 25cm/10in round. Press into the tins, cover with a dampened dish cloth and leave for 30 minutes to rise.

6 Make deep holes, about 2.5cm/ 1in apart, in the dough. Cover and leave for a further 20 minutes.

7 Scatter with the onions and drizzle over the oil. Sprinkle with the salt. then a little cold water, to stop a crust from forming.

8 Bake for about 25 minutes, sprinkling with water again during cooking. Cool on a wire rack.

PAPPARDELLE WITH OLIVE AND CAPER PASTE

This home-made pasta is flavoured with sun-dried tomato paste. The results are well worth the effort, but bought pasta can be substituted for a really quick supper dish.

FOR THE PASTA
275g/10oz/2½ cups plain white flour
1.5ml/¼ tsp salt
3 size 2 eggs
45ml/3 tbsp sun-dried tomato paste

FOR THE SAUCE
115g/4oz/⅔ cup pitted black olives
75ml/5 tbsp capers
5 drained anchovy fillets
1 red chilli, seeded and roughly chopped
60ml/4 tbsp roughly chopped basil
60ml/4 tbsp roughly chopped parsley
150ml/¼ pint/⅔ cup olive oil
4 ripe tomatoes
salt and ground black pepper
flat leaf parsley or basil, to garnish
Parmesan cheese shavings, to serve

SERVES 4

1. To make the pasta, sift the flour and salt into a bowl and make a well in the centre. Lightly beat the eggs with the tomato paste and pour the mixture into the well.

2. Mix the ingredients together using a round-bladed knife. Turn out on to a work surface and knead for 6–8 minutes until the dough is very smooth and soft, working in a little more flour if it becomes sticky. Wrap in aluminium foil and chill for 30 minutes.

3. To make the sauce, put the olives, capers, anchovies, chilli, basil and parsley in a food processor or blender with the oil. Process very briefly until the ingredients are finely chopped. (Alternatively, you can finely chop the ingredients and then mix with the olive oil.)

4. Plunge the tomatoes into boiling water for 30 seconds, then refresh in cold water. Peel away the skins, remove the seeds and dice. Roll out the dough very thinly on a floured surface. Sprinkle with a little flour, then roll up like a Swiss roll. Cut across into 1cm/½ in slices.

5. Unroll the pasta and lay out on a clean dish towel for about 10 minutes to dry out.

6. Bring a large saucepan of salted water to the boil. Add the pasta and cook for 2–3 minutes until just tender. Drain immediately and return to the saucepan.

7. Add the olive mixture, tomatoes and salt and black pepper to taste, then toss together gently over a moderate heat for about 1 minute until heated through. Garnish with parsley or basil and serve scattered with Parmesan shavings.

SPANISH ONION AND ANCHOVY PIZZA

This pizza has flavours and ingredients brought to Spain by the Moors and still used today in many classic Spanish recipes.

400g/14oz/2½ cups strong plain flour
2.5ml/½ tsp salt
15g/½oz easy-blend dried yeast
120ml/4fl oz/½ cup olive oil
150ml/¼ pint/⅔ cup milk and water,
in equal quantities, mixed together
3 large onions, thinly sliced
50g/2oz can anchovies, drained and
roughly chopped
30ml/2 tbsp pine nuts
30ml/2 tbsp sultanas
5ml/1 tsp dried chilli flakes or powder
salt and ground black pepper

SERVES 6–8

1   Sift the flour and salt together into a large bowl. Stir in the yeast. Make a well in the centre, and add 60ml/4 tbsp of the olive oil, and a little of the milk and water. Bring the flour mixture and liquid together, gradually adding the remaining milk and water, until a dough is formed. Knead on a floured surface for about 10 minutes. Return to the bowl, cover with a cloth, and leave in a warm place to rise for about 1 hour.

2   Heat the remaining oil in a large frying pan, add the onions, and cook until soft. Preheat the oven to 240°C/475°F/Gas 9.

3   Knock back the dough, and roll out to a rectangle about 30 x 38cm/12 x 15in. Place on an oiled baking sheet. Cover with the onions. Scatter over the anchovies, pine nuts, sultanas and chilli flakes. Season. Bake for 10–15 minutes, until the edges are beginning to brown. Serve hot.

MUSHROOM AND PESTO PIZZA

Home-made Italian-style pizzas are a little time-consuming to make but the results are well worth the effort.

FOR THE PIZZA BASE
*350g/12oz/3 cups strong plain flour
1.5ml/¼ tsp salt
15g/½oz easy-blend dried yeast
15ml/1 tbsp olive oil*

FOR THE FILLING
*50g/2oz dried porcini mushrooms
25g/1oz/¾ cup fresh basil
25g/1oz/⅓ cup pine nuts
40g/1½oz Parmesan cheese, thinly
sliced
105ml/7 tbsp olive oil
2 onions, thinly sliced
225g/8oz chestnut mushrooms, sliced
salt and ground black pepper*

SERVES 4

1 To make the pizza base, put the flour in a bowl with the salt, dried yeast and olive oil. Add 250ml/8fl oz/1 cup hand-hot water and mix to a dough using a round-bladed knife.

2 Turn on to a work surface and knead for 5 minutes until smooth. Place in a clean bowl, cover with clear film and leave in a warm place until doubled in bulk.

3 Meanwhile, make the filling. Soak the dried mushrooms in hot water for 20 minutes. Place the basil, pine nuts, Parmesan and 75ml/5 tbsp of the olive oil in a blender or food processor and process to make a smooth paste. Set the paste aside.

4 Fry the onions in the remaining olive oil for 3–4 minutes until beginning to colour. Add the chestnut mushrooms and fry for 2 minutes. Stir in the drained porcini mushrooms and season lightly.

5 Preheat the oven to 220°C/425°F/Gas 7. Lightly grease a large baking sheet. Turn the pizza dough on to a floured surface and roll out to a 30cm/12in round. Place on the baking sheet.

6 Spread the pesto mixture to within 1cm/½in of the edges. Spread the mushroom mixture on top.

7 Bake the pizza for 35–40 minutes until risen and golden.

OLIVE BREAD

Olive breads are popular all over the Mediterranean. For this Greek recipe use rich oily olives or those marinated in herbs rather than canned ones.

2 red onions, thinly sliced
30ml/2 tbsp olive oil
225g/8oz/1⅓ cups pitted black or
green olives
750g/1¾lb/7 cups strong plain flour
7.5ml/1½ tsp salt
20ml/4 tsp easy-blend dried yeast
45ml/3 tbsp each roughly chopped
parsley, coriander or mint

MAKES TWO 675G/1½LB LOAVES

 Fry the onions in the oil until
soft. Roughly chop the olives.

 Put the flour, salt, yeast and
parsley, coriander or mint in a
large bowl with the olives and fried
onions and pour in 475ml/16fl oz/
2 cups hand-hot water.

VARIATION
Shape the dough into 16 small rolls.
Slash the tops as above and reduce
the cooking time to 25 minutes.

Mix to a dough using a round-
bladed knife, adding a little
more water if the mixture feels dry.

Turn out on to a lightly floured
surface and knead for about
10 minutes. Put in a clean bowl,
cover with clear film and leave in a
warm place until doubled in bulk.

Preheat the oven to 220°C/
425°F/Gas 7. Lightly grease two
baking sheets. Turn the dough on to a
floured surface and cut in half. Shape
into two rounds and place on the
baking sheets. Cover loosely with
lightly oiled clear film and leave until
doubled in size.

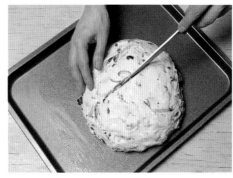

 Slash the tops of the loaves with
a knife then bake for about
40 minutes or until the loaves sound
hollow when tapped on the bottom.
Transfer to a wire rack to cool.

STUFFED KIBBEH

Kibbeh is a tasty North African speciality of minced meat and bulgur wheat.
The patties are sometimes stuffed with additional meat and deep fried.
Moderately spiced, they're good with yogurt or Cacik sauce.

450g/1lb lean lamb (or lean minced
lamb or beef)
oil for deep frying
avocado slices and coriander sprigs,
to serve

FOR THE KIBBEH
225g/8oz/1⅓ cups bulgur wheat
1 red chilli, seeded and
roughly chopped
1 onion, roughly chopped
salt and ground black pepper

FOR THE STUFFING
1 onion, finely chopped
50g/2oz/⅔ cup pine nuts
30ml/2 tbsp olive oil
7.5ml/1½ tsp ground allspice
60ml/4 tbsp chopped fresh coriander

SERVES 4–6

1 If necessary, roughly cut up the lamb and process the pieces in a blender or food processor until minced. Divide the minced meat into two equal portions.

2 To make the kibbeh, soak the bulgur wheat for 15 minutes in cold water. Drain well, then process in the blender or food processor with the chilli, onion, half the meat and plenty of salt and pepper.

3 To make the stuffing, fry the onion and pine nuts in the oil for 5 minutes. Add the allspice and remaining minced meat and fry gently, breaking up the meat with a wooden spoon, until browned. Stir in the coriander and a little seasoning.

4 Turn the kibbeh mixture out on to a work surface and shape into a cake. Cut into 12 wedges.

5 Flatten one piece in the palm of your hand and spoon a little stuffing into the centre. Bring the edges of the kibbeh up over the stuffing to enclose it. Make into a firm egg-shaped mould between the palms of the hands, ensuring that the filling is completely encased. Repeat with the other kibbeh.

6 Heat oil to a depth of 5cm/2in a large pan until a few kibbeh crumbs sizzle on the surface.

7 Lower half the kibbeh into the oil and fry for about 5 minutes until golden. Drain on kitchen paper and keep them hot while cooking the remainder. Serve with avocado slices and coriander sprigs.

EGYPTIAN RICE WITH LENTILS

*...ith spices in many ways in the Middle East and two important staples come together
in this dish, which can be served hot or cold.*

*350g/12oz/1½ cups large brown
lentils, soaked overnight in water
2 large onions
45ml/3 tbsp olive oil
15ml/1 tbsp ground cumin
2.5ml/½ tsp ground cinnamon
225g/8oz/generous 1 cup
long grain rice
salt and ground black pepper
flat leaf parsley, to garnish*

SERVES 6

1 Drain the lentils and put in a
large pan. Add enough water to
cover by 5cm/2in. Bring to the boil,
cover and simmer for 40 minutes to
1½ hours, or until tender. Drain
thoroughly.

2 Finely chop one onion, and
slice the other. Heat 15ml/1 tbsp
oil in a pan, add the chopped onion
and fry until soft. Add the lentils, salt,
pepper, cumin and cinnamon.

3 Measure the volume of rice and
add it, with the same volume of
water, to the lentil mixture. Cover and
simmer for about 20 minutes, until
both the rice and lentils are tender.
Heat the remaining oil in a frying pan,
and cook the sliced onion until very
dark brown. Tip the rice mixture into
a serving bowl, sprinkle with the
onion and serve hot or cold,
garnished with flat leaf parsley.

BAKED CHEESE POLENTA WITH TOMATO SAUCE

*Polenta, or cornmeal, is a staple food in Italy. It is cooked like a sort of porridge, and eaten soft, or set,
cut into shapes then baked or grilled.*

5ml/1 tsp salt
250g/9oz/2¼ cups quick-cook polenta
5ml/1 tsp paprika
2.5ml/½ tsp ground nutmeg
30ml/2 tbsp olive oil
1 large onion, finely chopped
2 garlic cloves, crushed
2 x 400g/14oz cans chopped tomatoes
15ml/1 tbsp tomato purée
5ml/1 tsp sugar
salt and ground black pepper
75g/3oz Gruyère cheese, grated

SERVES 4

1 Preheat the oven to 200°C/
400°F/Gas 6. Line a baking tin
(28 x 18cm/11 x 7in) with clear film.
Bring 1 litre/1¾ pints/4 cups water to
the boil with the salt.

2 Pour in the polenta in a steady
stream and cook, stirring
continuously, for 5 minutes. Beat in
the paprika and nutmeg, then pour
into the prepared tin and smooth the
surface. Leave to cool.

3 Heat the oil in a pan and cook
the onion and garlic until soft.
Add the tomatoes, purée and sugar.
Season. Simmer for 20 minutes.

4 Turn out the polenta on to a
chopping board, and cut into
5cm/2in squares. Place half the
squares in a greased ovenproof dish.
Spoon over half the tomato sauce,
and sprinkle with half the cheese.
Repeat the layers. Bake for about
25 minutes, until golden.

...ITH SAFFRON AND PICKLED WALNUTS

...a warm, tangy flavour that is lovely in rice and bulgur wheat dishes. This Eastern
...pilaff is interesting enough to serve on its own or with grilled lamb or pork.

5ml/1 tsp saffron strands
40g/1½oz/½ cup pine nuts
45ml/3 tbsp olive oil
1 large onion, chopped
3 garlic cloves, crushed
1.5ml/¼ tsp ground allspice
4cm/1½in piece fresh root
ginger, grated
225g/8oz/generous 1 cup
long grain rice
300ml/½ pint/1¼ cups vegetable stock
50g/2oz/½ cup pickled walnuts,
drained and roughly chopped
40g/1½oz/¼ cup raisins
45ml/3 tbsp roughly chopped parsley
or fresh coriander
salt and ground black pepper
parsley or coriander, to garnish
natural yogurt, to serve

SERVES 4

1 Put the saffron in a bowl with 15ml/1 tbsp boiling water and leave to stand. Heat a large frying pan and dry-fry the pine nuts until they turn golden. Set them aside.

2 Heat the oil in the pan and fry the onion, garlic and allspice for 3 minutes. Stir in the ginger and rice and cook for 1 minute more.

3 Add the stock and bring to the boil. Reduce the heat, cover and simmer gently for 15 minutes until the rice is just tender.

4 Stir in the saffron and liquid, the pine nuts, pickled walnuts, raisins and parsley or coriander. Season to taste with salt and pepper. Heat through gently for 2 minutes. Garnish with parsley or coriander leaves and serve with natural yogurt.

VARIATION
Use one small aubergine, chopped and fried in a little olive oil, instead of the pickled walnuts, if you prefer.

RISOTTO ALLA MILANESE

Italian risottos have a distinctive creamy texture that is achieved by using arborio rice, a short grain rice which absorbs plenty of stock, but at the same time retains its texture. This risotto, scattered with cheese and gremolata, makes a delicious light meal or accompaniment to a meaty stew or casserole.

FOR THE GREMOLATA
2 garlic cloves, crushed
60ml/4 tbsp chopped fresh parsley
finely grated rind of 1 lemon

FOR THE RISOTTO
5ml/1 tsp (or 1 sachet) saffron strands
25g/1oz/2 tbsp butter
1 large onion, finely chopped
*275g/10oz/1½ cups arborio
(risotto) rice*
150ml/¼ pint/⅔ cup dry white wine
*1 litre/1¾ pints/4 cups chicken or
vegetable stock*
salt and ground black pepper
Parmesan cheese shavings

SERVES 4

1 To make the gremolata, mix together the garlic, parsley and lemon rind and reserve.

2 To make the risotto, put the saffron in a small bowl with 15ml/1 tbsp boiling water and leave to stand. Melt the butter in a heavy-based saucepan and gently fry the onion for 5 minutes.

3 Stir in the rice and cook for about 2 minutes until it becomes translucent. Add the wine and saffron mixture and cook for several minutes until the wine is absorbed.

4 Add 600ml/1 pint/2½ cups of the stock to the pan and simmer gently until the stock is absorbed, stirring frequently.

5 Gradually add more stock, a ladleful at a time, until the rice is tender. (The rice might be tender and creamy before you've added all the stock so add it slowly towards the end of the cooking time.)

6 Season the risotto with salt and pepper and transfer to a serving dish. Scatter lavishly with shavings of Parmesan cheese and the gremolata.

VARIATION
If preferred, stir plenty of grated Parmesan cheese into the risotto.

SPICED VEGETABLE COUSCOUS

Couscous, a cereal processed from semolina, is used throughout North Africa, mostly in Morocco, where it is served with meat, poultry and Moroccan vegetable stews or tagines.

45ml/3 tbsp vegetable oil
1 large onion, finely chopped
2 garlic cloves, crushed
15ml/1 tbsp tomato purée
2.5ml/½ tsp ground turmeric
2.5ml/½ tsp cayenne pepper
5ml/1 tsp ground coriander
5ml/1 tsp ground cumin
225g/8oz/1½ cups cauliflower florets
225g/8oz baby carrots, trimmed
1 red pepper, seeded and diced
4 beefsteak tomatoes
225g/8oz/1¾ cups courgettes, thickly sliced
400g/14oz can chick-peas, drained and rinsed
45ml/3 tbsp chopped fresh coriander
salt and ground black pepper
coriander sprigs, to garnish

FOR THE COUSCOUS
5ml/1 tsp salt
450g/1lb/2⅔ cups couscous
50g/2oz/2 tbsp butter

SERVES 6

1 Heat 30ml/2 tbsp of the oil in a large pan, add the onion and garlic, and cook until soft. Stir in the tomato purée, turmeric, cayenne, ground coriander and cumin. Cook, stirring, for 2 minutes.

2 Add the cauliflower, carrots and pepper, with enough water to come halfway up the vegetables. Bring to the boil, then lower the heat, cover and simmer for 10 minutes.

COOK'S TIP
Beefsteak tomatoes have excellent flavour and are ideal for this recipe, but you can substitute six ordinary tomatoes or two 400g/14oz cans chopped tomatoes.

3 Plunge the tomatoes into boiling water for 30 seconds, then refresh in cold water. Peel away the skins and chop. Add the sliced courgettes, chick-peas and tomatoes to the other vegetables and cook for a further 10 minutes. Stir in the fresh coriander and season with salt and pepper. Keep hot.

4 To cook the couscous, bring 475ml/16fl oz/2 cups water to the boil in a large saucepan. Add the remaining oil and the salt. Remove from the heat, and add the couscous, stirring. Allow to swell for 2 minutes, then add the butter, and heat through gently, stirring to separate the grains.

5 Turn the couscous out on to a warm serving dish, and spoon the vegetables on top, pouring over any liquid. Garnish and serve.

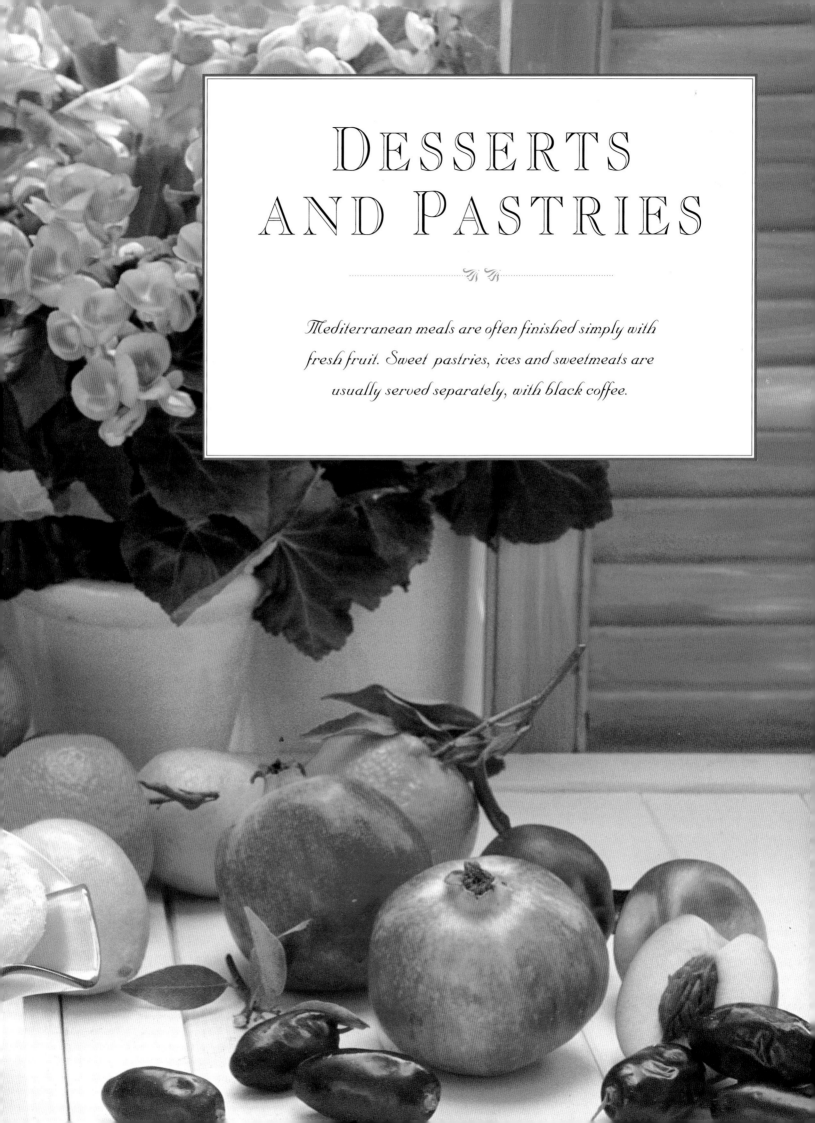

DESSERTS AND PASTRIES

Mediterranean meals are often finished simply with fresh fruit. Sweet pastries, ices and sweetmeats are usually served separately, with black coffee.

A peep in the glass display cabinets of any pâtisserie, confectioner or coffee house just about anywhere around the Mediterranean will reveal an absolute feast of sweet treats. From highly decorated gâteaux and torte, lavishly finished with sugared decorations, to the painstakingly stuffed and glazed or candied fruits, all Mediterranean sweets thrive on an abundance of fabulous flavours. Many desserts, pastries and sweetmeats involve complex cookery techniques and need specialized ingredients, and they are perhaps best left to the skills of professional pastry chefs! These include some of the lavish, multi-flavoured ice cream gâteaux of Italy and a number of the specialized pastries of the Arab world.

On a domestic level most Mediterranean desserts take full advantage of the glorious abundance of fresh fruits. For a special occasion a colourful selection of seasonal fruits such as figs, plums, apricots, peaches, melons and cherries make a stunning finale. These can be arranged on a platter lined with vine or fig leaves, some fruits cut open decoratively, and the whole platter scattered with crushed ice. On a simpler scale, the flesh of juicy fruits such as pomegranates or sweet oranges can be arranged in bowls, sprinkled with sugar and rosewater or orange

BELOW: Orange groves abound in this fertile valley near Jaén in Spain.

ABOVE: Plump, rosy and ready for picking, peaches make a perfect dessert, alone or with a delicious amaretto stuffing.

ABOVE: Pyramids of perfect fruit await the shopper at the covered market in Florence.

flower water and served iced. Fresh fruits can also be lightly poached in sugar or honey-sweetened syrups, sometimes with the addition of mild spices. They'll store well for several days as the syrup becomes impregnated with the delicious flavours of the fruit and spices. Pears, quinces, apricots and figs are typical examples. Other refreshing desserts are the smooth sorbets of France and the granitas of Italy, or the grilled or baked fruits which are so full of flavour. Sometimes these are sugared or topped with a scoop of mascarpone or ricotta and laced with a little liqueur. A selection of dried fruits, available in abundance and of good quality, makes an ideal end to a meal, when served with dessert wine or liqueurs.

In Turkey, Greece, Lebanon and Egypt, small sweet pastries and sweetmeats are enjoyed as a between-meal snack with good strong coffee. These include the rich pastries, doughnuts, and semolina and nut cakes, drenched in spiced syrup and featuring flavours like honey, almonds, pistachios, sesame, pine nuts, rose-water and orange flower water. Served in small pieces, they make a wonderful contrast to the bitterness of the coffee. The Semolina and Nut Halva is a light version of a syrupy steeped cake which makes it perfect with coffee, or as a dessert with cream.

Other prominent Mediterranean desserts are the sweet milk-based puddings of both the east and the west. In North Africa and the Middle East these are made with ground or short grain rice and spiced with cinnamon, cloves, aniseed or fennel. They are usually served cold, sometimes drizzled with a honey and orange flavoured syrup. One of Spain's classic puddings is the moreish Crema Catalana, a sweet creamy dessert that is absolutely delicious either on its own or accompanied by fresh or sweetened fruits.

FRESH FIGS WITH HONEY AND WINE

Any variety of figs can be used in this recipe, their ripeness determining the cooking time. Choose ones that are plump and firm, and use quickly as they don't store well.

450ml/¾ pint/1⅞ cups dry white wine
75g/3oz/⅓ cup clear honey
50g/2oz/¼ cup caster sugar
1 small orange
8 whole cloves
450g/1lb fresh figs
1 cinnamon stick
mint sprigs, or bay leaves, to decorate

FOR THE CREAM
300ml/½ pint/1¼ cups double cream
1 vanilla pod
5ml/1 tsp caster sugar

SERVES 6

[1] Put the wine, honey and sugar in a heavy-based saucepan and heat gently until the sugar dissolves.

[2] Stud the orange with the cloves and add to the syrup with the figs and cinnamon. Cover and simmer very gently for 5–10 minutes until the figs are softened. Transfer to a serving dish and leave to cool.

[3] Put 150ml/¼ pint/⅔ cup of the cream in a small saucepan with the vanilla pod. Bring almost to the boil, then leave to cool and infuse for 30 minutes. Remove the vanilla pod and mix with the remaining cream and sugar in a bowl. Whip lightly. Transfer to a serving dish. Decorate the figs, then serve with the cream.

CHURROS

These Spanish doughnuts are commercially deep fried in huge coils and broken off into smaller lengths for selling. Serve this home-made version freshly cooked with hot chocolate or strong coffee.

200g/7oz/1¾ cups plain flour
1.5ml/¼ tsp salt
30ml/2 tbsp caster sugar
60ml/4 tbsp olive or sunflower oil
1 egg, beaten
caster sugar and ground cinnamon
for dusting
oil for deep frying

MAKES 12–15

1 Sift the flour, salt and sugar on to a plate or piece of paper. Heat 250ml/8fl oz/1 cup water in a saucepan with the oil until it boils.

2 Tip in the flour mixture and beat with a wooden spoon until the mixture forms a stiff paste. Leave to cool for 2 minutes.

3 Gradually beat in the egg until smooth. Oil a large baking sheet. Sprinkle plenty of sugar on to a plate and stir in a little cinnamon.

4 Put the dough in a large piping bag fitted with a 1cm/½in plain piping nozzle. Pipe little coils or "s" shapes on to the baking sheet.

5 Heat 5cm/2in of oil in a large pan to 168°C/336°F or until a little dough sizzles on the surface.

6 Using an oiled fish slice, lower several of the piped shapes into the oil and cook for about 2 minutes until light golden.

7 Drain on kitchen paper then coat with the sugar and cinnamon mixture. Cook the remaining churros in the same way and serve immediately.

WALNUT AND RICOTTA CAKE

Soft, tangy ricotta cheese is widely used in Italian sweets. Here, it is included along with walnuts and orange to flavour a whisked egg sponge. Don't worry if it sinks slightly after baking — this gives it an authentic appearance.

115g/4oz/1 cup walnut pieces
150g/5oz/²⁄₃ cup unsalted butter, softened
150g/5oz/²⁄₃ cup caster sugar
5 eggs, separated
finely grated rind of 1 orange
150g/5oz/²⁄₃ cup ricotta cheese
40g/1½oz/6 tbsp plain flour

TO FINISH
60ml/4 tbsp apricot jam
30ml/2 tbsp brandy
50g/2oz bitter or plain chocolate, coarsely grated

MAKES 10 SLICES

1 Preheat the oven to 190°C/ 375°F/Gas 5. Grease and line the base of a deep 23cm/9in round, loose-based cake tin. Roughly chop and lightly toast the walnuts.

2 Cream together the butter and 115g/4oz/½ cup of the sugar until light and fluffy. Add the egg yolks, orange rind, ricotta cheese, flour and walnuts and mix together.

3 Whisk the egg whites in a large bowl until stiff. Gradually whisk in the remaining sugar. Using a large metal spoon, fold a quarter of the whisked whites into the ricotta mixture. Carefully fold in the rest of the whisked whites.

4 Turn the mixture into the prepared tin and level the surface. Bake for about 30 minutes until risen and firm. Leave the cake to cool in the tin.

5 Transfer the cake to a serving plate. Heat the apricot jam in a small saucepan with 15ml/1 tbsp water. Press through a sieve and stir in the brandy. Use to coat the top and sides of the cake. Scatter the cake generously with grated chocolate.

VARIATION
Use toasted and chopped almonds in place of the walnuts.

BISCOTTI

These lovely Italian biscuits are part-baked, sliced to reveal a feast of mixed nuts and then baked again until crisp and golden. Traditionally they're served dipped in Vin Santo, a sweet dessert wine - perfect for rounding off a Mediterranean meal.

50g/2oz/¼ cup unsalted butter,
softened
115g/4oz/½ cup caster sugar
175g/6oz/1½ cups self-raising flour
1.5ml/¼ tsp salt
10ml/2 tsp baking powder
5ml/1 tsp ground coriander
finely grated rind of 1 lemon
50g/2oz/½ cup polenta
1 egg, lightly beaten
10ml/2 tsp brandy or orange-
flavoured liqueur
50g/2oz/½ cup unblanched almonds
50g/2oz/½ cup pistachio nuts

MAKES 24

1 Preheat the oven to 160°C/ 325°F/Gas 3. Lightly grease a baking sheet. Cream together the butter and sugar.

2 Sift all the flour, salt, baking powder and coriander into the bowl. Add the lemon rind, polenta, egg and brandy or liqueur and mix together to make a soft dough.

3 Stir in the nuts until evenly combined. Halve the mixture. Shape each half into a flat sausage about 23cm/9in long and 6cm/2½in wide. Bake for about 30 minutes until risen and just firm. Remove from oven.

4 When cool, cut each sausage diagonally into 12 thin slices. Return to the baking sheet and cook for a further 10 minutes until crisp.

5 Transfer to a wire rack to cool completely. Store in an airtight tin for up to 1 week.

COOK'S TIP
Use a sharp, serrated knife to slice the cooled biscuits, otherwise they will crumble.

SEMOLINA AND NUT HALVA

Semolina is a popular ingredient in many desserts and pastries in the Eastern Mediterranean. Here it provides a spongy base for soaking up a deliciously fragrant spicy syrup.

1 Preheat the oven to 220°C/ 425°F/Gas 7. Grease and line the base of a deep 23cm/9in square solid-based cake tin.

2 Lightly cream the butter in a bowl. Add the sugar, orange rind and juice, eggs, semolina, baking powder and hazelnuts and beat the ingredients together until smooth.

3 Turn into the prepared tin and level the surface. Bake for 20–25 minutes until just firm and golden. Leave to cool in the tin.

4 To make the syrup, put the sugar in a small heavy-based saucepan with 575ml/18fl oz/2¼ cups water and the half cinnamon sticks. Heat gently, stirring, until the sugar has dissolved completely.

5 Bring to the boil and boil fast, without stirring, for 5 minutes. Measure half the boiling syrup and add the lemon juice and orange flower water to it. Pour over the halva. Reserve the remainder of the syrup in the pan.

6 Leave the halva in the tin until the syrup is absorbed then turn it out on to a plate and cut diagonally into diamond-shaped portions. Scatter with the nuts.

7 Boil the remaining syrup until slightly thickened then pour it over the halva. Scatter the shredded orange rind over the cake and serve with lightly whipped or clotted cream.

FOR THE HALVA
115g/4oz/½ cup unsalted butter, softened
115g/4oz/½ cup caster sugar
finely grated rind of 1 orange, plus 30ml/2 tbsp juice
3 eggs
175g/6oz/1 cup semolina
10ml/2 tsp baking powder
115g/4oz/1 cup ground hazelnuts

TO FINISH
350g/12oz/1½ cups caster sugar
2 cinnamon sticks, halved
juice of 1 lemon
60ml/4 tbsp orange flower water
50g/2oz/½ cup unblanched hazelnuts, toasted and chopped
50g/2oz/½ cup blanched almonds, toasted and chopped
shredded rind of 1 orange

SERVES 10

COOK'S TIP
Be sure to use a deep solid-based cake tin, rather than one with a loose base, otherwise the syrup might seep out.

CREMA CATALANA

...g is a cross between a crème caramel and a crème brûlée. It is not as rich
...e brûlée, but has a similar caramelized sugar topping.

475ml/16fl oz/2 cups milk
pared rind of ½ lemon
1 cinnamon stick
4 egg yolks
105ml/7 tbsp caster sugar
25ml/1½ tbsp cornflour
ground nutmeg

SERVES 4

1 Put the milk in a pan with the lemon rind and cinnamon stick. Bring to the boil, then simmer for 10 minutes. Remove the lemon peel and cinnamon. Place the egg yolks and 45ml/3 tbsp of the sugar in a bowl, and whisk until pale yellow. Add the cornflour and mix well.

2 Stir in a few tablespoons of the hot milk, then add this mixture to the remaining milk. Return to the heat and cook gently, stirring, for about 5 minutes, until thickened and smooth. Do not let it boil. There should be no cornflour taste.

3 Pour into 4 shallow ovenproof dishes, about 13cm/5in in diameter. Leave to cool, then chill for a few hours, overnight if possible, until firm. Before serving, sprinkle each pudding with a tablespoon of sugar and a little of the ground nutmeg. Preheat the grill to high.

4 Place the puddings under the grill, on the highest shelf, and cook until the sugar caramelizes. This will only take a few seconds. Leave to cool for a few minutes before serving. (The caramel will only stay hard for about 30 minutes.)

MOROCCAN RICE PUDDING

A simple and delicious alternative to a traditional rice pudding. The rice is cooked in almond-flavoured milk and delicately flavoured with cinnamon and orange flower water.

25g/1oz/¼ cup blanched almonds, chopped
450g/1lb/2¼ cups pudding rice
25g/1oz/¼ cup icing sugar
7.5cm/3in cinnamon stick
50g/2oz/¼ cup butter
pinch salt
1.5ml/¼ tsp almond essence
175ml/6fl oz /¾ cup milk
175ml/6fl oz/¾ cup condensed milk
30ml/2 tbsp orange flower water
toasted flaked almonds and ground cinnamon, to decorate

SERVES 6

1 Put the almonds in a food processor or blender with 60ml/4 tbsp of very hot water. Process, then push through a sieve into a bowl. Return to the food processor or blender, add a further 60ml/4 tbsp very hot water, and process again. Push through the sieve into a saucepan.

2 Add 300ml/½ pint/1¼ cups water to the almond "milk" and bring to the boil. Add the rice, sugar, cinnamon and half the butter, the salt, the almond essence, and half the milk. (Mix the milks together.)

3 Bring to the boil, then simmer, covered, for about 30 minutes, adding more milk if necessary. Continue to cook the rice, stirring, and adding the remaining milk, until it becomes thick and creamy. Stir in the orange flower water, then taste the rice pudding for sweetness, adding extra sugar, if necessary.

4 Pour the rice pudding into a serving bowl, and sprinkle with the flaked almonds. Dot with the remaining butter and dust with ground cinnamon. Serve hot.

TURKISH DELIGHT ICE CREAM

Not strictly a traditional Middle Eastern recipe, but a delicious way of using Turkish delight.
Serve scattered with rose petals, if you have them.

4 egg yolks
115g/4oz/½ cup caster sugar
300ml/½ pint/1¼ cups milk
300ml/½ pint/1¼ cups double cream
15ml/1 tbsp rose water
175g/6oz rose-flavoured Turkish delight, chopped

SERVES 6

 1 Beat the egg yolks and sugar until light. In a pan, bring the milk to the boil. Add to the egg and sugar, stirring, then return to the pan.

2 Continue stirring over a low heat until the mixture coats the back of a spoon. Do not boil, or it will curdle. Leave to cool, then stir in the cream and rose water.

3 Put the Turkish delight in a pan with 30–45ml/2–3 tbsp water. Heat gently, until almost completely melted, with just a few small lumps. Remove from the heat and stir into the cool custard mixture.

4 Leave the mixture to cool completely, then pour into a shallow freezer container. Freeze for 3 hours until just frozen all over. Spoon the mixture into a bowl.

5 Using a whisk, beat the mixture well, and return to the freezer container and freeze for 2 hours more. Repeat the beating process, then return to the freezer for about 3 hours, or until firm. Remove the ice cream from the freezer 20–25 minutes before serving. Serve with thin almond biscuits or meringues.

ICED ORANGES

These little sorbets served in the fruit shell were originally sold in the beach cafés in the south of France. They are pretty and easy to eat — a good picnic treat to store in the cold box.

150g/5oz/⅔ cup granulated sugar
juice of 1 lemon
14 medium oranges
8 fresh bay leaves, to decorate

SERVES 8

1 Put the sugar in a heavy-based pan. Add half the lemon juice, and 120ml/4fl oz/½ cup water. Cook over a low heat until the sugar has dissolved. Bring to the boil, and boil for 2–3 minutes, until the syrup is clear. Leave to cool.

2 Slice the tops off eight of the oranges, to make "hats". Scoop out the flesh of the oranges, and reserve. Put the empty orange shells and "hats" on a tray and place in the freezer until needed.

3 Grate the rind of the remaining oranges and add to the syrup. Squeeze the juice from the oranges, and from the reserved flesh. There should be 750ml/1¼ pints/3 cups. Squeeze another orange or add bought orange juice, if necessary.

4 Stir the orange juice and remaining lemon juice, with 90ml/6 tbsp water into the syrup. Taste, adding more lemon juice or sugar, as desired. Pour the mixture into a shallow freezer container and freeze for 3 hours.

5 Turn the mixture into a bowl, and whisk to break down the ice crystals. Freeze for 4 hours more, until firm, but not solid.

6 Pack the mixture into the orange shells, mounding it up, and set the "hats" on top. Freeze until ready to serve. Just before serving, push a skewer into the tops of the "hats" and push in a bay leaf.

COOK'S TIP
Use crumpled kitchen paper to keep the shells upright.

STUFFED PEACHES WITH MASCARPONE CREAM

Mascarpone is a thick velvety Italian cream cheese, made from cow's milk. It is often used in desserts, or eaten with fresh fruit.

4 large peaches, halved and stoned
40g/1½oz amaretti biscuits, crumbled
30ml/2 tbsp ground almonds
45ml/3 tbsp sugar
15ml/1 tbsp cocoa powder
150ml/¼ pint/⅔ cup sweet wine
25g/1oz/2tbsp butter

FOR THE MASCARPONE CREAM
30ml/2 tbsp caster sugar
3 egg yolks
15ml/1 tbsp sweet wine
225g/8oz/1 cup mascarpone cheese
150ml/¼ pint/⅔ cup double cream

SERVES 4

3 Place the peaches in a buttered ovenproof dish and fill them with the stuffing. Dot with the butter, then pour the remaining wine into the dish. Bake for 35 minutes.

4 To make the mascarpone cream, beat the sugar and egg yolks until thick and pale. Stir in the wine, then fold in the mascarpone. Whip the double cream to soft peaks and fold into the mixture. Remove the peaches from the oven and leave to cool. Serve at room temperature, with the mascarpone cream.

1 Preheat the oven to 200°C/400°F/Gas 6. Using a teaspoon, scoop some of the flesh from the cavities in the peaches, to make a reasonable space for stuffing. Chop the scooped-out flesh.

2 Mix together the amaretti, ground almonds, sugar, cocoa and peach flesh. Add enough wine to make the mixture into a thick paste.

CHERRY CLAFOUTIS

When fresh cherries are in season this makes a deliciously simple dessert for any occasion. Serve warm with a little pouring cream.

675g/1½lb fresh cherries
50g/2oz/½ cup plain flour
pinch of salt
4 eggs, plus 2 egg yolks
115g/4oz/½ cup caster sugar
600ml/1 pint/2½ cups milk
50g/2oz/¼ cup melted butter
caster sugar for dusting

SERVES 6

1 Preheat the oven to 190°C/ 375°F/Gas 5. Lightly butter the base and sides of a shallow ovenproof dish. Stone the cherries and place in the dish.

2 Sift the flour and salt into a bowl. Add the eggs, egg yolks, sugar and a little of the milk and whisk to a smooth batter.

3 Gradually whisk in the rest of the milk and the rest of the butter, then strain the batter over the cherries. Bake for 40–50 minutes until golden and just set. Serve warm, dusted with caster sugar, if you like.

VARIATION
Use 2 x 425g/15oz cans stoned black cherries, thoroughly drained, if fresh cherries are not available. For a special dessert, add 45ml/3 tbsp kirsch to the batter.

COFFEE GRANITA

Granitas are like semi-frozen sorbets, but consist of larger particles of ice. Served in Italian cafés, they are very refreshing, particularly in the summer. Some are made with fruit, but the coffee version is perhaps the most popular and is often served with a spoonful of whipped cream on top.

350ml/12fl oz/1½ cups hot strong espresso coffee
30ml/2 tbsp sugar
250ml/8fl oz/1 cup double cream
10ml/2 tsp caster sugar

SERVES 6–8

1 Stir the sugar into the hot coffee until dissolved. Leave to cool, then chill. Pour into a shallow plastic or metal freezer container, cover and freeze for about 1 hour.

2 The coffee should have formed a frozen crust around the rim of the container. Scrape this away with a spoon and mix with the rest of the coffee. Repeat this process every 30 minutes, using the spoon to break up the clumps of ice.

3 After about 2½ hours, the granita should be ready. It will have the appearance of small, fairly uniform ice crystals. Whip the cream with the caster sugar until stiff. Serve the granita in tall glasses, each topped with a spoonful of cream.

DATE AND ALMOND TART

Fresh dates make an unusual but delicious filling for a tart. The influences here are French and Middle Eastern — a true Mediterranean fusion!

FOR THE PASTRY
175g/6oz/1½ cups plain flour
75g/3oz/6 tbsp butter
1 egg

FOR THE FILLING
90g/3½oz/scant ½ cup butter
90g/3½oz/7 tbsp caster sugar
1 egg, beaten
90g/3½oz/scant 1 cup ground almonds
30ml/2 tbsp plain flour
30ml/2 tbsp orange flower water
12–13 fresh dates, halved and stoned
60ml/4 tbsp apricot jam

SERVES 6

1 Preheat the oven to 200°C/ 400°F/Gas 6. Place a baking sheet in the oven. Sift the flour into a bowl, add the butter and work with your fingertips until the mixture resembles fine breadcrumbs. Add the egg and a tablespoon of cold water, then work to a smooth dough.

2 Roll out the pastry on a lightly floured surface and use to line a 20cm/8in tart tin. Prick the base with a fork, then chill until needed.

3 To make the filling, cream the butter and sugar until light, then beat in the egg. Stir in the ground almonds, flour and 15ml/1 tbsp of the orange flower water, mixing well.

4 Spread the mixture evenly over the base of the pastry case. Arrange the dates, cut side down, on the almond mixture. Bake on the hot baking sheet for 10–15 minutes, then reduce the heat to 180°C/350°F/Gas 4. Bake for a further 15–20 minutes until light golden and set.

5 Transfer the tart to a rack to cool. Gently heat the apricot jam, then press through a sieve. Add the remaining orange flower water.

6 Brush the tart with the jam and serve at room temperature.

LEMON TART

This is one of the classic French desserts, and it is difficult to beat. A rich lemon curd, encased in crisp pastry. Crème fraîche is an optional accompaniment.

3 Roll the pastry out on a floured surface, and use to line a 23cm/9in tart tin. Line with foil or greaseproof paper and fill with dried beans or rice, or baking beans if you have them. Bake for 10 minutes.

FOR THE PASTRY
225g/8oz/2 cups plain flour
115g/4oz/½ cup butter
30ml/2 tbsp icing sugar
1 egg
5ml/1 tsp vanilla essence

FOR THE FILLING
6 eggs, beaten
350g/12oz/1½ cups caster sugar
115g/4oz/½ cup unsalted butter
grated rind and juice of 4 lemons
icing sugar for dusting

SERVES 6

1 Preheat the oven to 200°C/ 400°F/Gas 6. Sift the flour into a bowl, add the butter, and work with your fingertips until the mixture resembles fine breadcrumbs. Stir in the icing sugar.

4 To make the filling, put the eggs, sugar and butter into a pan, and stir over a low heat until the sugar has dissolved completely. Add the lemon rind and juice, and continue cooking, stirring all of the time, until the lemon curd has thickened slightly.

2 Add the egg, vanilla essence and a scant tablespoon of cold water, then work to a dough.

5 Pour the mixture into the pastry case. Bake for 20 minutes, until just set. Transfer the tart to a wire rack to cool. Dust with icing sugar just before serving.

HONEY AND PINE NUT TART

Wonderful tarts of all descriptions are to be found throughout France, and this recipe recalls the flavours of the south.

FOR THE PASTRY
225g/8oz/2 cups plain flour
115g/4oz/½ cup butter
30ml/2 tbsp icing sugar
1 egg

FOR THE FILLING
115g/4oz/½ cup unsalted butter, diced
115g/4oz/½ cup caster sugar
3 eggs, beaten
175g/6oz/⅔ cup sunflower or other flower honey
grated rind and juice of 1 lemon
225g/8oz/2⅔ cups pine nuts
pinch of salt
icing sugar for dusting

SERVES 6

1. Preheat the oven to 180°C/ 350°F/Gas 4. Sift the flour into a bowl, add the butter and work with your fingertips until the mixture resembles fine breadcrumbs. Stir in the icing sugar. Add the egg and 15ml/1 tbsp of water and work to a firm dough that leaves the bowl clean.

3. Cream together the butter and caster sugar until light. Beat in the eggs one by one. Gently heat the honey in a small saucepan until runny, then add to the butter mixture with the lemon rind and juice. Stir in the pine nuts and salt, then pour the filling into the pastry case.

2. Roll out the pastry on a floured surface and use to line a 23cm/9in tart tin. Prick the base with a fork, and chill for 10 minutes. Line with foil or greaseproof paper and fill with dried beans or rice, or baking beans if you have them. Bake the tart shell for 10 minutes.

4. Bake for about 45 minutes, until the filling is lightly browned and set. Leave to cool slightly in the tin, then dust generously with icing sugar. Serve warm, or at room temperature, with crème fraîche or vanilla ice cream.

GLAZED PRUNE TART

Generously glazed, creamy custard tarts are a pâtisserie favourite all over France. Plump prunes, heavily laced with brandy or kirsch, add a wonderful taste and texture to this deliciously sweet and creamy filling.

225g/8oz/1 cup ready-to-eat prunes
60ml/4 tbsp brandy or kirsch

FOR THE SWEET PASTRY
175g/6oz/1½ cups plain flour
pinch of salt
115g/4oz/½ cup unsalted butter
25g/1oz/2 tbsp caster sugar
2 egg yolks

FOR THE FILLING
150ml/¼ pint/⅔ cup double cream
150ml/¼ pint/⅔ cup milk
1 vanilla pod
3 eggs
50g/2oz/¼ cup caster sugar

TO·FINISH
60ml/4 tbsp apricot jam
15ml/1 tbsp brandy or kirsch
icing sugar for dusting

SERVES 8

1 Put the prunes in a bowl with the brandy or kirsch and leave for about 4 hours until most of the liqueur has been absorbed.

2 To make the pastry, sift the flour and salt into a bowl. Add the butter, cut into small pieces, and rub in with the fingertips. Stir in the sugar and egg yolks and mix to a dough using a round-bladed knife.

3 Turn the dough out onto a lightly floured surface and knead to a smooth ball. Wrap closely and chill for 30 minutes.

4 Preheat the oven to 200°C/400°F/ Gas 6. Roll out the pastry on a lightly floured surface and use to line a 24–25cm/9½–10in loose-based flan tin.

5 Line with greaseproof paper and fill with dried beans or rice, or baking beans if you have them. Bake for 15 minutes. Remove the beans and paper and bake for a further 5 minutes.

6 Arrange the prunes, evenly spaced, in the pastry case, reserving any liqueur left in the bowl.

7 For the filling, put the cream and milk in a saucepan with the vanilla pod and bring to the boil. Turn off the heat and leave the mixture to infuse for 15 minutes.

8 Whisk together the eggs and sugar in a bowl. Remove the vanilla pod from the cream and return the cream to the boil. Pour over the eggs and sugar, whisking to make a smooth custard.

9 Cool slightly then pour the custard over the prunes. Bake the tart for about 25 minutes until the filling is lightly set and turning golden around the edges.

10 Press the apricot jam through a sieve into a small pan. Add the liqueur and heat through gently. Use to glaze the tart. Serve warm or cold, dusted with icing sugar.

COOK'S TIP
The vanilla pod can be washed and dried, ready for using another time. Alternatively, use 5ml/1 tsp vanilla or almond essence.

INDEX

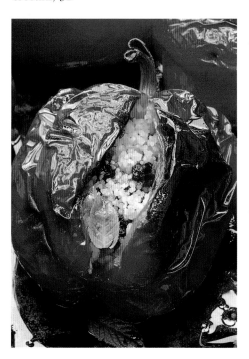

INDEX

Photographs: With the exceptions noted below, all photographs by Michelle Garrett:
Patrick McLeavey: p.10 (top right): The Image Bank: p.1, p.9 (bottom left), p.20 (top left),
p.108 (left), p.198, p.227 (right); The Anthony Blake Photo Library: p.9 (top right), p.138,
p.139, p.171 (top right), p.171 (bottom left), p.227 (left); Robert Estall: p.2, p.6–7, p.8;
Michael Busselle: p.87, p.170, p.226